TONY HILLERMAN
NEW MEXICO
RIO GRANDE
AND OTHER ESSAYS

Photography by David Muench and Robert Reynolds

Tony Hillerman

HarperPerennial
A Division of HarperCollinsPublishers

Books by Tony Hillerman

Fiction

Coyote Waits
Talking God
A Thief of Time
Skinwalkers
The Ghostway
The Dark Wind
People of Darkness
Listening Woman
Dance Hall of the Dead
The Fly on the Wall
The Blessing Way
The Boy Who Made Dragonfly *(for children)*
The Leaphorn Mysteries
The Chee Mysteries

Nonfiction

The Great Taos Bank Robbery
New Mexico
Rio Grande
The Spell of New Mexico
Indian Country
The Best of the West
Hillerman Country
Talking Mysteries
New Mexico/Rio Grande and Other Essays

page i: White Sands, Robert Reynolds; page ii: Rio Grande Gorge, David Muench;
page v: Acoma, Robert Reynolds; page vi: Kokopelli, David Muench

A hardcover edition of this book was published in 1992 by Graphic Arts Center Publishing Company. It is here reprinted by arrangement with Graphic Arts Center Publishing Company.

First HarperPerennial edition published 1993.
Designed by Robert Reynolds
Library of Congress Catalog Card Number 92-56249
ISBN 0-06-097558-X

93 94 95 96 97   SP   10 9 8 7 6 5 4 3 2 1

CONTENTS

New Mexico, Rio Salado Sands, David Muench

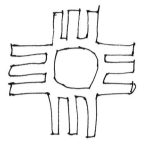

Often it begins in the late afternoon. A great bank of fog builds along the ridges of the Sandia Mountains, forming an opaque wall. It looms eventually a thousand feet higher than the ten-thousand-foot crest. Then it begins to spill—like the heavy vapor from a beaker of acid rolling down the glass.

From Albuquerque's West Mesa residential districts across the Rio Grande one sees it in perspective—a Niagara of fog pouring slowly down the cliffs of the mountain range. But for those who live on Albuquerque's northeastern fringes, in the Sandia foothills, this spectacle takes place almost directly overhead. The cataract of mist falls silently toward their roofs as if some great aerial dam had broken to pour down the clouds. The fog rarely reaches the foothills. Somewhere up the slope the warm air on the west face of the mountain reaches a balance with the cold mist pressing downward. The cloud begins to evaporate, ravelling away from the bottom. Then the red light of sunset catches all this and turns it pink. And what had been awe-inspiring is reduced to mere beauty.

This eye-catching phenomenon warns the central Rio Grande Valley—where almost half of New Mexico's people live—that the weather is changing. The Great Plains air mass east of the Sandia and Manzano mountains has become colder (or warmer) than the Colorado Plateau air west of the mountains. Two of the edges which meet in New Mexico are rubbing together.

It seems to those of us who live in New Mexico and try to understand her that many edges meet in this most peculiar of the fifty states. In meeting they give her climate, landscape, and society their character. It is here that the Rocky Mountains finally end in a chaos of parallel ridges. Here the Great Plains lap at last against the edge of these mountains. And here the Chihuahuan Desert — spread over an immensity of Mexico — is finally overcome by too much altitude and too many late summer thunderstorms. No other state offers such an abrupt contrast in landscape. Six of the continent's seven biological life zones are found within her borders — ranging down from the cold and windy arctic-alpine country above timberline to the sometimes torrid Lower Sonoran Desert.

New Mexico also lies under the edges of the forces which shape the American climate. It is too far west to get more than the weak fringe of the wet Gulf Stream air, and too many mountain ranges east to feel the full effects of the Pacific Westerlies, and on the very boundary of those great arctic blizzards which bulge down out of Canada across the nation's midlands. The net effect of location and altitude is a sort of cancellation — a climate basically dry, mild and dominated by the sun. The thin, dry air moderates the summer's heat, and almost constant sunlight warms the winters.

Something like this might also be said about its culture. Its population, too, has been formed by edges and overlappings — the meetings of migrations which had lost their force with cultures which had lost their intolerance.

We know little of the first who came — only that they were passing through on a southward migration away from the glaciers and toward the sun. A few remained and became the cultures we call the Cochise, and the Mogollon, and the Mimbres. From them came the Anasazi — the Old Ones — who built great apartment-style pueblos, and made beautiful pottery and formidable magic, and provided the roots of the first sophisticated civilization in what would become the United States. Around this peaceful communal pueblo civilization lapped the exhausted edges of later migrations.

The Athabascans came at the tag end of their long struggle down from the north — they were still strong enough to harass these peaceful farmers but too weak to overwhelm them. And so the Athabascans stayed, and learned and became the Navajos and the Apaches. The next wave were the Spanish — the last spasm of expansion of a dying empire. Had the Spanish arrived a little earlier, the peaceful culture of farmers would likely have been erased even more thoroughly than was that of the mighty Aztec. But these were milder conquistadores, representing a worn-out empire softened by internal decay and by the spreading philosophy of a saint called Francis of Assisi. Finally all of this was engulfed by the westward sweep of the Anglo-Americans. But without the magnet of material wealth to attract it, even Manifest Destiny lost force and ferocity here and allowed other cultures to survive. For once, the American melting pot failed to operate. New Mexico produced a mosaic of cultures instead of a mixture.

Always, as far back as geologists can read earth's history in its rocks, what is now New Mexico has been a place of margins and meetings. Here, a billion-and-a-half years ago, the lifeless Precambrian Ocean washed against the headlands of the still-dead continent. Its ebb and flow built layers of iron-rich silt which now streak the western cliffs of Caballo Mountain and the eastern escarpment of the San Andres Range. Down through the eons, as the planet aged and its oceans rose and fell with the shifting crust, fate made this the pattern for what would be New Mexico. The Ordovician Ocean made it an island and left behind immense deposits of limestone. The Silurian Sea, swarming with huge water scorpions and primitive fishes, lapped across its beaches and laid down layers of fossil-rich dolomite. In the Devonian era New Mexico was again on the margin of land and ocean — an immense steaming lowland of fern forests. On its fringes the coral grew and died and now forms the great bioherm mounds (some up to 350 feet high) in the Sacramento Mountains. The Mississippian and Pennsylvanian periods came and produced coal and oil, and then the Permian. Southern New Mexico sank under a great inland sea surrounded by incredible barrier reefs. Geologists call these reefs the Capitan and Goat Seep. From them, in subsequent millions of years, percolating water would dissolve away the world's largest sub-surface cavities, which we call the Carlsbad Caverns. Later, perhaps two hundred million years ago, the ocean gate closed and what had been open water became an inland sea. It stretched from Santa Fe southward over much of southeastern New Mexico — teeming with marine life, alternately drying under the searing sun and flooding with the changing climate. Gradually the land rose, draining the ocean southeastward until only the extreme southeastern corner of the state remained under the sea. The Age of Dinosaurs came, bringing to New Mexico principally the amphibian reptiles—the eighty-five-foot-long, fifty-ton Brachiosaurus, the ponderous Stegosaurus and a dazzling variety of others, which left their bones to be quarried in truck loads from the cliffs of Rio Arriba County.

New Mexico's landscape began taking its modern shape in what geologists call the Laramide Revolution—that paroxysm which shook the earth about twenty-five million years ago. New Mexico rose above sea level to stay tilted as it is today, from northwest to southeast. Southwestern New Mexico spouted and boiled with volcanoes building the Mogollon plateau. To the east, volcanic eruptions pushed Sierra Blanca twelve thousand feet into the sky. Mount Taylor, the Turquoise Mountain of the Navajos, was formed by another of these Neogene eruptions, as were Shiprock and most of the similar volcanic necks which dot the state's western half. In the south, the Tularosa Arch collapsed in one of nature's major cataclysms. A highland the size of Connecticut sank almost a mile, converting a mountain massif into a hundred-mile-long depression. The mountain ranges which rim it now were once its foothills. Very late in this period of recurrent volcanism—perhaps a mere million years ago—the earth produced a spectacle which gives New Mexico one of its most unusual features—the Valle Grande Caldera.

Eons of volcanic activity had formed the Jemez Mountains along the western edge of the Rio Grande trough. And over this mountain range towered what some geologists believe must have been the largest volcanic peak on the continent. (Some guess it was as tall as twenty-five thousand feet.) The same forces which built it soon destroyed it.

The first explosions opened vents on the northeastern face of the mountain—blasting millions of tons of melted rock miles into the air and spreading a layer of ash as far north and east as Oklahoma and Kansas. Then another hole opened on the east side of the volcano from which gushed an ash flood up to two hundred fifty feet deep. What was left of the mountain then destroyed itself. Other eruptions spread a blanket of burned rock up to one thousand feet deep over the surrounding plateau. With an estimated twenty-five cubic miles of its inside spewed into the atmosphere, the volcano collapsed into itself. What had been one of the greatest peaks in the hemisphere sank into a cavity twelve miles in diameter and as much as thirty-five hundred feet deep. (The eruption of Krakatoa Volcano, the largest explosion recorded by man on this planet, left a crater four miles across and two thousand feet deep.) Geologists say this caldera rivals one in Siberia as the largest on earth. It is now a great bowl of grass, a rancher's summer pasture.

If one stands in the fir-aspen forests which rim this bowl, the cattle which graze far below seem smaller than natural—out of scale with a setting. The bowl is simply too large for the eye to credit, and this odd optical effect is heightened by the transparent high-altitude air which robs the scene of the proper sense of dim blue distance.

It is, in fact, this thin, dry, clear air which gives New Mexico and the Southern Rocky Mountain highlands much of their unusual visual character. Passengers on west-bound flights over the state can hardly fail to notice the phenomenon. The Great American midlands they have crossed have been, in most seasons, at least partially hidden by an opaque layer of clouds. What landscape is open to view is made dim and hazy by a layer of low altitude air which is heavy with humidity. This layer of haze thins as the land rises to become the "High Plains" of Texas. Across the New Mexico border, the land gains altitude, steadily emerging from this hazy layer like the headland of a continent rising from a shelving sea. The dimness is gone, the softness, the haze. Ahead, to the north and to the south, the mountains are stark outlines in the harsh, clear light, their eastern slopes still packed with the winter's snow. The air is no longer translucent. It is transparent.

Part of this effect, of course, is a matter of moisture. Or lack of it. Albuquerque will average only eight inches of rain a year (compared with thirty-four inches at Dallas and Kansas City and Cleveland, and forty-four at Charleston, Norfolk, Tacoma, Wilmington and Baltimore, and sixty-eight at Mobile). But much of it is altitude. The troposphere loses one-thirtieth of its density with each nine hundred feet of altitude gained. New Mexico has been lifted an average of fifty-seven hundred feet above the oceans which once lapped across it. Its lowest point (in the extreme southwestern corner of the state) is a thousand feet higher than the loftiest peak in the Missouri Ozarks. One who gazes from the campus of St. John's

College at Santa Fe across the Rio Grande Valley toward Los Alamos looks through air which has lost a fourth of its weight. It is low in oxygen, low in carbon dioxide and high in hydrogen. It offers little to diffract or diffuse the light. Thus, the white buildings of the Los Alamos Scientific Laboratory, more than thirty miles away, are etched sharply against the dark green background of ponderosa pines. Thus, the lights of a New Mexico city seen from a distance are robbed of the soft and charming glow that belongs to humid lands. Instead they are a hundred thousand pinpoints of brilliance etched in the darkness. Here, the eye trained to milder light is deceived by distances, by horizons which stretch away one hundred fifty miles. Citizens of this arid tableland find themselves oppressed by lower climates. The low country sky closes them in, and gives them something like claustrophobia, and makes them yearn for the mountains.

Except for that strip of "Little Texas" oil country on the extreme southeastern margin of New Mexico, no part of the state is without its mountains. They range from the Animas to the Zunis — from the Bears, Big Burros and the Broke Offs, to the Victorios, Tularosas and Tres Hermanas — in all, seventy-three ranges and three hundred ten peaks are found worthy of naming on the better maps. Seven of the summits tower more than thirteen thousand feet above sea level, and eighty-five are at least two miles high. Most of them are arranged in ragged, north-south ridges, dominated by their own long-exhausted volcanic peaks, and dominating, in turn, the valleys into which their snowpack drains. On the average, they are less massive than the Northern Rockies, somewhat lower, older, with part of the rawness eroded away by eons of time and weather.

In the north, they bulge down across the Colorado border, rising from the high tableland of the Colorado Plateau. The greatest range is the Sangre de Cristo, named by the Spanish for the Blood of Christ because the peaks turn red at sunset. These wall off the upper Rio Grande Valley on the east. West of the river the rampart is formed by the ancient Nacimientos and the Jemez Range. Beyond them to the west lie the Ceboletas and the Chuskas. To New Mexicans, these form the "Northern Mountains." In general, they are higher, and the snow remains in sheltered east-slope notches until the very end of summer.

The Southern Mountains are lower, principally because they rise from a lower base. Here their feet are planted in the desert—the Tularosa Basin or the Plains of San Agustin. While they tower as much as a mile above surrounding terrain, the net altitude is less, and so is the amount of moisture they collect.

More than any other feature, it is the ubiquitous mountains that influence life in New Mexico. They collect nearly all the state's scanty moisture—building up snow packs from October through May and releasing it through the summer to fill irrigation ditches down in the valleys of the Rio Grande, and the Pecos, and the San Juan. On late summer afternoons, warm updrafts build towers of clouds miles into the sky over their high ridges. These thunderheads produce their pyrotechnic lightning (and a measles rash of forest fires) and drift eastward, trailing brief, noisy rain showers over the valleys. From Santa Fe, one can sometimes see as many as five such thundershowers simultaneously—one rumbling over the Sangre de Cristos, one obscuring Los Alamos and the Jemez Range with sheets of rain, another forming an immense pile of white a hundred miles away over Mount Taylor, and the others trailing curtains of thundershower over the Manzanos and across these rugged little out-croppings which New Mexicans call—with bilingual redundancy—"the Cerrillos Hills." Indians of the Rio Grande pueblos call these displays "male rains" in ironic reference to their high ratio of noise and visual display to the low level of moisture produced. "Female rains" are the much rarer general storms which bless the state now and then with fruitful, quiet, gentle precipitation. It's not unusual to have three male rains drift across Albuquerque on a single (and generally sunny) afternoon, leaving narrow strips of the city drenched but most of it still totally dry. The storms are products of mountain updrafts, which push the thin air too high in the stratosphere to hold its moisture.

In early mornings, the same mountains produce downdrafts which bring air from the forests and the meadows down into the streets of town. Early risers smell the scent of pine resin, and blue lupine, and nameless wild things. In New Mexico, the mountains affect the climate of the valleys, and the climate of the soul.

A scant one million people live in New Mexico, which is the fifth-largest state. Its 121,666 square miles equal the combined land area of Maine, New Hampshire, Vermont, Massachusetts, Rhode Island, Connecticut, New York, New Jersey, Maryland, and Delaware. The population, if spread evenly, would average out to a bit more than eight people per square mile (the national average is fifty-eight per mile). But people can live only where there is water. Thus, this million live clustered in a sort of oasis civilization— leaving most of the country almost totally empty.

Approximately a third of New Mexico's citizens occupy the four hundred square miles of Greater Albuquerque and its environs. More than half live in a narrow, irrigated belt down the Rio Grande. The remainder are clustered mostly in the northwestern and southwestern corners, where petroleum industries have flourished and where the Pecos and San Juan rivers pump irrigation water and provide enough moisture for a small farming industry. The "section line" pattern of the American farm belt, which divides the land into tidy mile-square places, each with its households, is made impossible here by the arid climate.

Those who value such misanthropic favors find that New Mexico can still bestow the gift of isolation. It is still easy to be alone. Even from the very heart of the state's major population center— Albuquerque's Northeast Heights shopping district— the pressures of civilization are eased by the knowledge that escape is near. From the noisy traffic jam at Menaul and Louisiana Boulevard, it's only minutes away to the immense, grassy emptiness of the West Mesa, or the spruce and aspen forests of the Sandias, or the shady cottonwood bosques of the Rio Grande bottoms— each offering its own variety of silence.

The first men to come were hunters. Their ancestors had come from Asia, following the mastodon and musk ox over what was then a land bridge from Siberia. They had drifted southward, escaping the ice, following the migration routes of the now-extinct mammals on which they preyed. And, being nomads, they left little more trace of their passing than did the dire wolves and the sabertoothed cats which hunted with them. Of their early interglacial migration, a clear-cut trace of only one camp has been found.

Crude stone tools, a roughly shaped lance tip, and the cooked bones of Ice age animals were left on the floor of Sandia Cave. Torrential rains of the glacial periods leached ochre out of the cliff and covered these remains with a thick yellow deposit. This, and the fact that the hunter had been toasting the bones of the long-vanished North American horse, camel, and giant ground sloth, have caused his presence to be dated back as early as twenty-five thousand years. Until something earlier is found, this Sandia Man can be called the First American.

We know almost nothing about him. The mouth of the cave he chose—a deep hole high on the wall of Las Huertas Canyon on the northeast slope of Sandia Mountain—commands a breathtaking view. One can see down-canyon all the way across the Rio Grande Valley to the Jemez Range. And across the canyon, there's the great forested slope of Sandia Mountain with puffy summer clouds dragging their bottoms through the spruce at its crest. This might suggest an appreciation of beauty. But perhaps he was driven here by danger. Neither the wolves nor the saber-tooth cats could reach this lofty perch.

Those who came later left more tracks to read. A large band of hunters trapped a family of mammoths in a bog near Clovis, on New Mexico's eastern plains, and left a tell-tale wealth of broken weapons and worn butchering tools among the bones. Anthropologists called them Clovis Man and dated them some thirteen thousand years before present. Their hunting methods, their large leaf-shaped lance points, and stone-working techniques have since been detected at Ice Age kill sites up and down the east slope of the Rockies. After Clovis Man came Folsom, who stampeded a herd of long-horned bison into a swamp near the village of Folsom, New Mexico, and killed thirteen of them, and left amid their bones the thin, fluted, "Folsom Points" which represent Stone Age America's most beautiful weaponry. This Folsom culture survived until perhaps nine thousand years ago, leaving scores of hunting camps buried under the grama grass on the plains which overlook the Rio Grande Valley. After him came other hunters, killing with larger, cruder lance points. Finally, civilization began.

Civilization seems to have begun about the same time on the western side of the Mogollon Plateau where southern New Mexico joins Arizona, and on the Colorado Plateau in the barren "Four Corners" where Colorado, Utah, Arizona, and New Mexico touch. The hunters had become foragers, gatherers of seeds, makers of baskets in which to store and carry foods. The highly portable skin shelters in which Folsom Man lived gave way to permanent pit houses as the nomad became farmer, planting domesticated seeds and harvesting corn and squash. By the time of Christ, the Hohokam people had developed effective irrigation systems of the Gila and Mimbres rivers in southwestern New Mexico, and the Anasazi were diverting arroyo floods with sophisticated damming systems into cornfields of northwestern New Mexico. From their pit houses they moved above ground, devising building techniques which used cut stones and puddled adobe. They also developed an art for ceramics, weaving, pictographs, and petroglyphs.

The cultures which developed from these roots were rich and varied. They prospered in the period when Europe groaned through the bloody autocratic chaos of the Dark Ages, and they flowered into what the cultural historians call the Golden Age of the Pueblos. New Mexico, plus Colorado and Arizona where they adjoin its northwestern borders, is dotted with literally thousands of ruins left by these people—most of them still unexcavated.

By early in the twelfth century, Pueblo Bonito in Chaco Canyon had been built into a five-story stone apartment complex of eight hundred rooms and a three-acre floor plan. Some five thousand persons lived in this community, their religious and medicine clans using thirty-two ceremonial kivas, and their farmlands watered by an extensive system of arroyo dams. Other such centers flourished in Frijoles Canyon just below the modern site of Los Alamos, at Mesa Verde, and elsewhere.

These pueblo-dwellers evolved a sophisticated cultural system based on trade, assigned duties, and social responsibilities. They developed art—music and dance as well as visual. They devised a form of government which came closer to modern democratic ideals than did the Athens of Pericles. Most important of all, they developed a philosophy which survives into the twentieth century and is part of the flavor of modern New Mexico.

While European and Middle Eastern civilization saw man as lord of the universe, the center of nature, the reason for all creation, the Pueblo philosophers saw themselves and their brothers as parts of nature. Their happiness and well-being depended upon remaining in harmony with birds and beasts, sky and stone. Duty, health and fulfillment lay — not in the egocentric European concept of personal ambition, individual attainment, and material acquisition, but in such values as generosity, brotherhood, and the proper performance of the role to which one's clan, kiva, and pueblo had assigned him. There has never been a civilization quite like it. It was free, hospitable, and peaceful. In the face of what was coming it was, quite literally, too good to last. Yet, in many ways it did last. It survives today in the nineteen Pueblo tribes of modern New Mexico — and in the influence it has had on the successive migrations which were to lap around it.

The next to come were the Athabascans — the people who would become the Navajos and the Apaches of the Southwest, and the Iroquois of Canada and the Eastern woodlands, and the complex fishing civilizations of the Pacific Northwest. But as was its pattern, New Mexico was on the fringe of this human wave. Only a trickle reached the Southern Rockies — little bands of stragglers who lived hungrily off the land. We guess at most of what happened. They raided the peaceful Pueblo communities and stole from them and were awed by their civilization and by the magic of these people who could, with their prayer plumes and their ritual dances, call the clouds across the sky, and make rain fall. Most of these new-comers learned to plant and harvest, ended their wanderings, and became the Navajos, calling themselves Diné, "The People," and their cousins, who rejected the sedentary life, Apaches. In Navajo, the word means "enemy."

Perhaps the arrival of the Athabascans ended the Golden Age of Pueblo building. Most likely it was many things. We know that the people who now occupy Cochiti Pueblo made several of their community's six moves during this period. We know that after abandoning their great pueblo of Tyuonyi in Frijoles Canyon, most of their new town sites were chosen for defense. But we also know a story tree rings have to tell us. In the summer of 1276 the magic of the kivas began to fail. The clouds no longer came at the call of the ritual dancers. The drought lasted unbroken for twenty-four consecutive years. There's been nothing like it since. And when it was ended, only the blowing dust moved in the last of the great pueblos of the Golden Age. The drought, perhaps augmented by diseases, seems to have pretty well depopulated New

Mexico. The survivors rebuilt their communities along the Rio Grande, and in the valleys of the Pecos and the Jemez, and at other lower sites where there was living water. And thus it remained until the edge of the next great human tide washed feebly into New Mexico from the south.

Had the invasion happened two or three generations earlier, it's not likely that the gentle Pueblo culture would have survived. But the little column of 130 soldiers, a few score families, and eighty-three ox carts of supplies which Don Juan de Oñate brought north from Chihuahua in 1598 was not the same sort of invasion that destroyed the Aztec empire, or tumbled the mighty Inca war machine into ruins. Oñate was not Cortéz, nor Pizarro, and the Spain of Philip II was very different from the Spain of Charles I.

The tide of the Spanish Empire was at flood, but the force was gone. Oñate's ramshackle little column winding northward from the Rio Grande ford at El Paso del Norte was part of the final spasm of expansion. Ten years earlier Queen Elizabeth's new fleet had destroyed the antiquated and outgunned Spanish navy in the English Channel and left the Duke of Alba's invincible army stranded in the Netherlands. The balance of power had shifted, but in terms of New Mexico history, it was more important that philosophy had softened the fanaticism of the conquistadores. Whatever mystical urge had inspired the incredible, ruthless destroying bravery of the conquests of Mexico and Peru had been infected. The Roman Catholic theologians had argued that American Indians were fellow humans, children of God, endowed with an immortal soul, and had caused the Spanish Crown to accept that position and decree that these pagans should be brought to Christianity — and not exterminated.

An older-fashioned conquistador, Francisco Vasquez de Coronado, had explored the territory a half century earlier, pursuing a myth of El Dorado, an Indian ruler who coated himself with gold, and the Seven Cities of Cibola, where gold was used as paving blocks. He had found, instead, the seven stone towns of Zuni, the Rio Grande civilization, and the emptiness of the Great Plains.

Coronado came for gold. Oñate's followers came to stay. They brought plows, seeds, sheep and axes, but few wives. Long exposure to the Moorish-Arabic culture had left them without

Northern Europe's racial bigotry. They would find wives among the Indians.

Looking at this tiny column through the perspective of history helps one understand why the Indian cultures in its path survived while those of eastern America did not. The English brought with them the concept of racial superiority and the metaphysics of Puritanism, Calvinism, and the idea of "salvation of the elect and damnation of the many." Among the English and the Dutch there were no niggling, time-wasting doubts and arguments about the Indians. Unless they got in the way, they were let alone. If the white man wanted their land, they were driven out or exterminated, with neither malice nor intended cruelty. Lord Amherst, representing the British Crown in the English colonies, suggested that smallpox be spread among the savages to clear the land for more rapid development by the Christians, but germ warfare had not yet been perfected and nothing came of the idea. The English colonists moved slowly and left no Indian cultures behind them. They would have found the expedition of Oñate hard to understand.

These Spanish marched, literally, under two flags — the Royal Pennant of the Spanish Crown and the banner of the Catholic Church. They pledged loyalty to "the two majesties — God and Emperor." Oñate was a soldier, but he was surrounded by seven members of the Order of Friars Minor — followers of St. Francis who preached the joy of poverty and the brotherhood of man. The column's military purpose was to found and protect a colony which would hold the territory for the king, but these Franciscans sought a harvest of Indian souls baptized in the name of Christ. And how could one preach the message of conversion to Indians if the Army drove them away? And how could the government enslave them after they had been made brothers-in-Christ? After the great Oñate died, this dichotomy of purpose would produce a crippling, century-long quarrel between church and state in New Mexico. But from the very beginning, it caused a special relationship between the Spanish and the dwellers of the pueblos.

Legend tells us Oñate's column exhausted its supplies south of Socorro in a strip of desert which maps still call Jornada del Muerto (Deadman's Route). The legend reports that the Indian pueblo upriver sent runners with baskets of corn to rescue the invaders.

Historians haven't confirmed this tale, but it fits with the Pueblo tradition of generous hospitality. Whether or not this gesture was made, the Pueblos generally accepted the Spanish and were willing to hear about Christianity. Oñate met with leaders of more than thirty pueblos at what is now Santo Domingo and received their allegiance to Spain. Then he moved upstream to the confluence of Rio Chama with the Rio Grande. He named this pueblo San Juan of the Gentlemen in recognition of its hospitality and made it New Mexico's first capital.

There was only a little fighting in this period in which New Mexico's Pueblo Indian culture became Spanish Pueblo. But it produced an epic feat of arms as awe-inspiring as the stand of Leonidas and his Spartan at Thermopylae. To appreciate the courage involved, you must see Acoma. And when you see it, it is almost impossible to believe this "sky city" fortress could have been stormed.

Acoma is a rock-and-adobe pueblo built atop an island of stone which juts 357 feet into the sky in the mesa country west of Albuquerque. Its top is irregular but almost level, seventy acres in size. A road has now been cut up its side, but in 1599, the only way to the top was via foot- and handholds cut into the cliffs. Originally, the Acomans had accepted the Spanish. But when Lieutenant Juan de Zaldívar paused there with a dozen men en route on a journey of explorations, they were invited up the cliffs and ambushed. Five of the thirteen fought their way to the edge of the precipice and jumped. Four somehow survived to take the tale of treachery to Oñate. A month later, Vicente de Zaldívar, the surviving nineteen-year-old brother of Juan, arrived with a punitive force of seventy men—more than half of the survivors of Oñate's army. Young Zaldívar left a dozen men to guard his horses and supplies and with the rest, fought his way, for three bloody days, up those cliffs, held by a mixed force of perhaps one thousand Acoma and Zuni warriors. Historian-anthropologist Charles Lummis, after examining the battleground, wrote this:

The forcing of that awful cliff, the three days' death struggle hand-to-hand, the storm of that fortress town room by savage room — time records nothing more desperately brilliant.

By 1628, when Oñate died, Spanish control was firmly established in the Rio Grande Valley and the mountains which overlook it. The capital was moved to Santa Fe in 1610, and mission churches were established in the various pueblos. The Pueblo Indians found the concepts of Christianity easy to adapt to their values of peace, brotherhood, and hospitality, and to their metaphysics of life-after-death, and a single all-powerful Creator, with benevolent interest in man. Even the "community of saints" concept of the Catholics was paralleled by their own idea of kachinas—the helpful ancestor spirits.

But the Spanish fought among themselves. The issues were old—the status of the Indians, and the conflict between church and state. It erupted repeatedly, with governors excommunicated as heretics and Franciscan missionaries jailed as criminal traitors. The Pueblo Indians eyed this dispute, suffering its effects. In 1680 they decided to throw out the white man and return to their old ways.

The revolt seems to have been planned largely in the Taos Pueblo—which even today is one of the more conservative. Its instigator was Popé, who tradition tells us had been forced to work in a Spanish mine near Cerrillos. Only Isleta just south of Albuquerque and the Piro "salt" Pueblos in the Manzano Mountains remained loyal to the Spanish. The rebels struck on the night of August 10, wiping out the Spanish in many of the outlying settlements in a single bloody night. The survivors were besieged in the Palace of the Governors in Santa Fe—the thick-walled building which forms one side of Santa Fe's central plaza. With their water supply exhausted, the colonists fought their way southward and, with aid from Isleta and Piro, reached El Paso. By year-end, the Indians were again masters of New Mexico.

The shaky Pueblo coalition quickly collapsed under the weight of Indian differences. The Spanish returned in 1692, under Don Diego de Vargas. Quickly and with little fighting, he restored Spanish control. (But the larger, better-armed force of De Vargas couldn't repeat young Zaldívar's conquest of Acoma. The Acomans held their fortress in the sky, then chose to accept Spanish control a year later.)

The story of the next 150 years for this northernmost of the Spanish colonies is one of poverty, government mismanagement and neglect, and sporadic combat between the Spanish and their Pueblo Indian allies on one hand, and Navajo, Apache and Comanche-Kiowa war parties on the other.

With the decline of Spain as a world power, its colonial administration rotted. This ultimate colony on the extreme northern frontier was virtually forgotten. It depended on a supply line which stretched more than two thousand miles from Mexico City. Its colonists had virtually no source of money to buy manufactured goods or weapons. Spanish (and later Mexican) policy restricted firearms to the military—and even the military was most often armed only with lance and bow. In the face of this weakness, an event of historic importance was taking place. The horse, imported by the Spanish, had been discovered by the Plains Indians, the Navajo and the Apache. A bloody new dimension was added to the struggle for the frontier. Through the eighteenth century the Spanish Pueblo civilization fought grimly for survival. Missions and pueblos and haciendas were abandoned. The Navajo pressed in from the northwest, the Apache from the south, and Comanche from the east. Colonial militiamen, often armed only with lances and bows, fought cavalry battles with Comanches armed with French-manufactured muskets. Population declined. Isolation increased. The fall of Spain to Napoleon was hardly noticed here. So far as Santa Fe was concerned, the Mexican war of independence did little more than change flags over the Palace of Governors. The bad situation became worse as the new Republic of Mexico tore itself apart with internal strife. Then from the east another wave of migration began to trickle toward the Southern Rocky Mountains.

Some historians believe that had not the Santa Fe Trail, which opened in 1821, given New Mexico an alternate supply line during this period, the colony and its Spanish-Pueblo civilization would have been erased by the raiding tribes. It seems equally likely that had New Mexico offered more material wealth, the forces of American "Manifest Destiny" would have crushed the existing cultures as thoroughly as they did in California and Texas. But once again New Mexico was on the margin.

Anglo-Americans had trickled into the territory early in the nineteenth century, drifting down from the Northern Rockies to trap beaver and do illegal trading. When the Santa Fe Trail brought regular wagon trains from Missouri, the trickle increased. The Mexican government, nervous about the intentions of its giant neighbor, officially prohibited admission of these trader-adventurers. Unofficially, the colony welcomed them for breaking the strangling monopoly held by Chihuahuan merchants on trade. Then the Mexican War flared in 1846, and the northern territory fell, virtually without resistance, into American hands.

The Treaty of Guadalupe Hidalgo and the subsequent Gadsden Purchase ceded all of what is now New Mexico to the United States. But here the traditional Anglo-American pattern of sweeping existing cultures away in the path of its westward march did not operate. There seemed to be almost nothing in this new territory which anyone wanted—a marginal farming economy principally operated by the Pueblo Indians, and a marginal cattle-sheep industry operated largely by the Spanish, a civilization of adobe villages scattered up the Rio Grande and its mountains, and a relentless and savage war with the nomadic Indians. There were at least two serious proposals that the United States should withdraw from this area and leave it to work out its own destiny. But the United States remained in authority and a third culture gradually super-imposed itself over the Indian and Spanish.

There were two brief revolts, at Taos and Mora, both put down by U.S. Army artillery fire. (The Taos Indians took refuge in their mission church and were slaughtered by cannons smashing its walls. The ruins still stand near the Taos Pueblo.) Then the U.S. Army took over from the Spanish-Pueblo forces the bloody job of fighting Navajos, Apaches, and Comanches. It proved to be the longest war in American history—lasting almost a half century.

The American Civil War brought a fourth flag to New Mexico. A Confederate column invading from Texas quickly captured federal forts in southern New Mexico, took Santa Fe, and then met Union forces in the fateful battle of Glorieta Pass east of the capital. Partly through luck, a force of Colorado volunteers found and captured the entire supply train of the Confederate army in Apache Canyon. The Southerners withdrew, evacuated Santa Fe, and retreated back to Texas. In 1863, the Navajo treaty was permanently broken by a midwinter scorched earth campaign. Colonel Kit Carson's troops slashed through the heartland of the

Diné in northwestern New Mexico and northeastern Arizona, chopping down orchards, burning food supplies and destroying hogans. Most of the Navajos surrendered and subsequently were moved to a concentration camp-reservation at Fort Sumner. There, after hunger and disease thinned their ranks, they signed a peace treaty and were allowed to return to a reservation carved out of part of their homeland. Fighting out of strongholds in the southern New Mexico mountains, the Apaches resisted for another quarter century, until Geronimo—the last war chief—surrendered to General Nelson Miles in 1886.

With the Kiowa-Comanche raiders penned on reservations in Oklahoma, the Navajos at peace, and the Apaches finally curbed, New Mexico's mining and cattle industries burgeoned. Millions of acres of almost virgin grassland were suddenly safe grazing for cattle. And the mountains, where the Apaches had made mining as dangerous as Russian roulette, were suddenly available for exploitation. There had been some gold and silver mining by the Spanish since early in the colonial period, and the Spanish had also opened the great copper deposits at Santa Rita. Now, prospectors swarmed into the mountains, and mining boomed. Ramshackle and rowdy camps sprouted in the Mogollons, the Black Range, the Jemez, the Sangre de Cristos, and elsewhere. Hillsboro, Kingston, Elizabethtown, Mogollon, Shakespeare, Golden, and a hundred other little towns flourished and died as the veins of ore were exhausted.

The mining boom was almost purely an Anglo-American affair, with little effect on the existing Spanish-Pueblo Indian cultures. The cattle boom was another matter.

On the plains country of New Mexico's east side, it was largely a matter of filling a vacuum. The Kiowa-Comanches had dominated this buffalo grass country since the horse had given them their mobility. Now they were gone, and their empire was quickly seized by Texas ranchers and land-hungry immigrants from the ruined Confederacy. Animosity between Texans and the Spanish/Mexican cultures had long since become traditional. Along the buffalo plains feelings had been especially embittered by the practice of Spanish "comancheros" trading with the Indians and buying from them cattle and horses stolen in Texas. A brutal reprisal raid by Texas freebooters through northwestern New Mexico had worsened relations. Most of the few Spanish who had survived in the risky area along the Texas border were quickly dispossessed in actions which gave New Mexico some of its immense ranch spreads, and its old Spanish colonial families their "grandfather stories" of murder and injustice. In New Mexico, to call a man a "Tejano" (Texan) is still an insult.

In the Rio Grande Valley and the high plateau of northern New Mexico, history took another turn. The land grant system, one of the most practical devices of the Spanish colonial system, collapsed under the weight of Anglo-American occupation. The reasons were complex and the results—for the Spanish farmer-ranchers—were disastrous.

The Spanish Crown (later, the Viceroy in Mexico City and still later, Mexican authorities), had granted ownership of large tracts of land to the community of people who would use it. The Spaniards blocked out the land being used by the Indian Pueblos and set it aside for them. Other large tracts of land were issued to towns, villages and sometimes to families. Individuals might own a small homesite in the village in their own right, but the entire village shared the right to water, to grazing for their cattle, to timber and firewood. Many of these grants were described in vague terms, since the territory had not been surveyed. At the insistence of the Mexican government, a clause was written into the Treaty of Guadalupe Hidalgo whereby the United States guaranteed to honor the rights of the Pueblo Indians and the Spanish colonists under these grants. But honor proved to be a void. With the American occupation, the corrupt Mexican administration in Santa Fe was replaced by an equally corrupt U.S. administration. Under it, the pioneers began losing their land to the newcomers.

What may have been a stupid accident made it easier. A U.S. territorial governor, trying to make an office available in the Palace of the Governors for the arrival of a U.S. Attorney cleaned out the Spanish Colonial Archives. Bales of priceless documents dating back to the sixteenth century were given away to be used as fuel. A deadline was set for the Spanish pioneers to file proof of their land ownership. It passed before many of them knew it. Others discovered the documents they needed had been burned, or were in Mexico City or Spain. Some of this land was placed in the public domain, eventually to become part of the national forest. Much of it went into private ownership—through forced sales for unpaid property tax (an institution imported by the Anglo-Americans) by questionable "purchases" of land grants from a grant heir, with the transaction then approved in a corrupt court, by fraudulent surveys, and other devices. With the so-called "Santa Fe Ring" controlling the federal bureaucracy and the territorial courts, resistance was fruitless. Nevertheless, there sometimes was resistance.

For example after Lucien Maxwell sold part of his holdings, described as "two million acres, more or less," to a European syndicate, the farmers and ranchers living on this expanse (almost half the size of Massachusetts) fought to avoid eviction from their lands. After four years of intermittent bloodshed the syndicate finally prevailed, aided by the law and hired Pinkerton gunmen. In southwestern New Mexico, the so-called "American Valley War" flared when owners associated with the Santa Fe Ring blocked off access to water through fraudulent homestead claims. And in east-central New Mexico, where John Chisum's one-hundred-fifty-square-mile kingdom of grass stretched from Texas to the White Mountains, the struggle flared into the Lincoln County War, with Billy the Kid killing seven of his twenty-one victims as a gunman for the losing side. By the end of the nineteenth century, little of the valuable land was left in the hands of the families who had tamed it. Thomas B. Catron, a former Confederate artillery captain who came to the territory fresh from a Union prisoner of war camp and became a key figure in both the Santa Fe Ring and territorial politics, had become America's largest land owner. By 1896, he controlled the 827,621-acre Mora Land Grant, the 584,515-acre Tierra Amarilla Grant, and at least five other grants plus extensive holdings elsewhere.

The twentieth century brought only relatively slow change to New Mexico. By 1912, when it became the forty-seventh state, its population had reached only three hundred thirty thousand, and its economy was still based on small farms, great ranches, and a mixed bag of mining—most notably the old Spanish workings at Santa Rita now developed into the immense open-pit Chino Mine by Kennecott Copper, coal in the northwest, and potash in the southeast. Early in the new century, artists had discovered the clear air. An art colony flourished first at Taos and then at Santa Fe, attracting writers, bohemians, rich eccentrics and assorted hangers-on. World War II accelerated the change. Robert Oppenheimer had attended the little Los Alamos Boys School on the Pajarito Plateau across the Rio Grande from Santa Fe. He remembered the empty isolation of the place when the time came to pick a site for building the atomic bomb. Thus, the Manhattan Project was moved to Los Alamos. What was to be a small hidden laboratory grew to be a scientific city of 15,000. The supporting Sandia Base and Laboratories at Albuquerque caused that city's population to soar from 35,500 in 1940 to 96,815 in 1950, to 201,190 in 1960, to an estimated 280,000 in 1974. Discovery of the free world's largest uranium deposits in the Ambrosia Lakes area west of Mount Taylor added a new dimension to the mining economy in the 1950s. Petroleum development boomed in the southeast corner of the state, and discovery of the great natural gas deposits in the northwest brought additional growth. But there is a limit to this growth. People require water, and water in New Mexico is scarce. Those who love the loneliness thank God for that.

U.S. Highway 64 runs westward—an asphalt line drawn ruler-straight through the sagebrush flats of the Taos Plateau. Behind you, an afternoon thunderstorm is building a top-heavy white tower over the Taos Mountains. To the northwest, another cloud has formed over the conical peak of San Antonio Mountain. Thirty miles ahead, the worn-down highlands of the ancient Brazos Range form a low, blue line. You drive through a wilderness of silver-grey sage, relieved here and there by clusters of juniper or pinon, or a meadow where the sickle blades of grama grass are blowing. Then, with breath-catching suddenness you are on the Rio Grande Gorge Bridge. The bridge, second-highest arch in the United States, soars two thousand feet from rim to rim. From eight hundred feet below, the sound of the river drifts upward. Here the river is hurrying, pouring down an endless series of falls, rapids, and narrows. Down among the slick black basalt boulders, the noise is loud and constant. But heard from the bridge, the voice of the river is muted by distance, inaudible when the breeze whines through the steel structures, and no more than a grumble when the breeze is stilled. It seems too small to have cut this great gorge and too small for its name. Yet it is the nation's second-longest river, extending 1,885 miles from its headwaters in the San Juan Mountains to its mouth in the Gulf of Mexico, draining a half-million square miles of Colorado, New Mexico, Texas and Mexico. And it is the aorta of New Mexico—the principal carrier of the water upon which more than half of the state's citizens depend. Under this bridge the water is clear and cold, fresh from melted snowpacks. Its deep pools are famous as the habitat of trophy-sized brown trout, but the steep and risky climb down the black cliffs restricts the fishing to those with sure feet and strong lungs. The sun reaches the bottom of this narrow slot only at midday, when it reflects hot and bright from the water-polished basalt. At other times, this is a cool, dim world of foam and spray, dark pools, with the world of men closed off by the constant lulling roar of falling water and the towering cliffs.

From the Colorado border southward past its junction with the Red River Canyon, the gorge has been declared one of America's "Wild Rivers" with its untouched character to be preserved. Below this junction, at the place where Taos Creek pours its cold contribution into the river, the Rio Grande assumes another of its many characters. Here it is still clear, but the canyon widens and access is easier. Past the old village of Pilar, it tumbles over another series of milder rapids, popular with white water rafters. (The death toll among them has averaged about one per year.) The gorge has become the Rio Grande Canyon, and at Velarde, the wild river is subjected to its first bridle. A diversion dam detours part of its water through the fields of the village.

New Mexico 68, which has followed the canyon much of the way from Taos into the Española Valley, skirts the old community on a hillside. The passerby looks down, in a sense, on the Spanish Colonial past. The tiny, compact village is a patchwork of apple, peach and cherry orchards, garden-sized fields of corn and chili, well-tended irrigation ditches, modest adobe homes—many tin-roofed here because of snow. Draw a hundred-mile circle around this village and you have the heart of what remains of America's Spanish Colonial culture. Truchas, Cundiyo, Chimayo, Santa Cruz, Talpa, Ranchos de Taos, Peñasco, Arroyo Seco, Arroyo Hondo, Rio Sarco and Ojo Sarco, Cordova, and Canjilon, Tierra Amarilla, El Valle, Llano, Rodarte—humble villages with proud names which once lined the northern frontier of the Spanish Empire. Each different and yet all alike. Most of them dating from the eighteenth century—some from the seventeenth and some from the nineteenth—and all bypassed by the twentieth. They are adobe villages, the color of the earth, peaked roofs against the high country snow or flat in valleys—and often sprouting weeds from their earthen insulation. In their way, Truchas and Las Trampas are typical. They were both built early in the eighteenth century to guard Sangre de Cristo mountain passes against the marauding Comanches. Truchas is a double line of adobe houses lining a windy cliff edge under the Truchas Peaks, and Las Trampas is a hollow square in the narrow valley of Rito las Trampas. They were there when George Washington was born. Truchas was founded by two families, and Trampas by a man named Juan de Arguello. Arguello was seventy-seven years old and a battle-scarred veteran of a long life of frontier wars when he led his sons-in-law and their families from Santa Fe to establish this lonely and dangerous new outpost. The chronicles report that when he was ninety-nine he walked over the mountains to the Peñasco Valley to ask donations for the village chapel. He died at 117. With the U.S. occupation, the village lost all its communal grazing lands. But Las Trampas lives on, terribly poor, and terribly proud of its church which is a lovely and priceless example of Spanish-Colonial architecture. If you understand Juan de Arguello, you can understand how a few hundred Spanish held this immense territory and why New Mexico Spanish-Americans are rooted to these northern mountains.

Below Velarde, the Rio Grande canyon opens into Española Valley. The river is wider here, and slower moving, its banks now shaded by the cottonwoods. In the late autumn, they make it a ribbon of bright yellow all the way to Mexico. Here it irrigates the fields of the San Juan, Santa Clara, and San Ildefonso Indians, and rides through the last of its rapids in White Rock Canyon, now orange with the silt of the Rio Chama. It funnels between the Santa Fe Plateau and the Pajarito Plateau, pouring past the mouths of the great canyons where many of the Pueblo Indians had their ancestral homes, and drops into the Santo Domingo Valley. Where the Pueblos of Santo Domingo and Cochiti have their reservations, the river is blocked by the Cochiti Dam, one of the world's largest earthen structures. This dam will collect silt and control floods. But at this level, the river has already been taken firmly in hand by the Bureau of Reclamation's Middle Rio Grande Irrigation District. At Albuquerque, where it waters a widening expanse of orchards and alfalfa fields, its bed is usually dry sand by mid-summer — its flow diverted into canals. The district stretches more than one hundred miles through central New Mexico — ending below the village of San Antonio. There the Rio Grande is sluggish, wandering through the San Marcial marshes in a stretch of country that man has never quite managed to tame.

In a way totally different from the noisy bottom of the Rio Grande Gorge, this stretch of river also offers escape from man. Here the generous Rio Grande withdraws its hospitality and cuts through barren country. The valley itself is more narrow and marshy than is true up-river. To the west are the Coyote Hills, carpeted with bunch-grass, cacti and creosote bush. Behind them lie the San Mateo Mountains, and behind the mountains, the vastness of the Plains of San Agustin. East of the river, the Jornada del Muerto, the stony, waterless plain which the Spanish feared, fills a twenty-mile gap amid the valley and dark shape of the Oscura Mountains. The emptiness of this landscape is certified by what lies beyond this ridge. Trinity Site. The place picked for detonation of the first atomic bomb. A community of Piro Indians tried this country, leaving a ruined pueblo to testify to their failure. The Spanish tried, and left only dots on the provincial maps. San Marcial, the settlement which gave its name to the marshes here, was wiped out twice by Rio Grande floods and permanently erased. Anglo-American latecomers established Clyde. A flood removed it.

The valley was given, in name, to Antonio Sandoval — the final land grant before American occupation. But it belonged to whoever was strong enough to hold it — and foolish enough to try. It's called Bosque del Apache because their raiding parties used its shady cottonwood groves for rest and recuperation.

Then John Chisum took it as part of his cattle empire. And finally, during the Great Depression, it fell into federal hands and became a wilderness area and the Bosque del Apache National Wildlife Refuge. It is the winter home for perhaps half a million birds and — except for the high mountain species — the entire index of Southwestern mammals.

The four lanes of Interstate 25 southbound from Albuquerque to El Paso leave the valley at Socorro and skirt through the foothills. Along the river there is only the narrow, abandoned pavement of what once was U.S. 85. Now the grass eats at the road's edges and sprouts through its cracks. If you stand beside your car here at dawn on a winter morning, and listen, and look, you can recapture how it was when the Apaches gave this place its name. The musical murmur on the still air is the conversation of birds—morning talk of tens of thousands of waterfowl, the odd fluting of sandhill cranes, the shrill note of red-winged blackbirds, and blended sounds of scores of other species. And then, about when the rim of the sun has put a bright red glow behind the Oscuras, there is the sound of wings. The snow geese are usually first, rising off the marsh ponds to fly upstream for their morning feeding. They swing to the west, a cloud of wings rising above the cottonwoods—not a swarming, disorderly blackbird rabble, but a kaleidoscope of a hundred shifting-but-orderly goose formations. Now the sunlight catches them, fifteen thousand great white birds sweeping past the gray velvet of the Coyote Hills, turning toward you. Then the sky overhead is filled with the clamor of an infinity of geese. You have looked through time and seen what America has lost.

Below the Bosque, the river pours into Elephant Butte Reservoir—the long lake which waters the canals of Elephant Butte Irrigation District. From here to its junction with the Texas-Mexican border, the river is simply a feeding system. It grows long fiber cotton, onions, lettuce, and crops as varied as geese and pecans. In the lower valley, the land is as tamed, lush, and ordered as anywhere in the nation. But seventy-five miles to the east, across the Organ Mountains, something called Lake Lucero has produced White Sands Desert and comes as close as our continent can to total lifelessness. The opposite extreme of New Mexico's vertical climatic spectrum—the ice and granite ridges high above timberline—gives an illusion of deadness. Even in August the air is frigid there, and nothing seems to grow or move. But the worn stone is stained with lichens, looking like gray scars, or blue velvet, or black stains depending on the variety, but nonetheless alive. And between the cracks, where freezing has produced a seedbed, every sunny place has its alpine sunflowers, or moss campion, or the tiny high-altitude gentians. The tough gray cold-climate grass is almost everywhere and, if you're patient, you'll see a goshawk against the dark sky and, far below at the upper fringes of forest, the blue-black flash of the stellar jay.

Northeast of Lake Lucero the illusion takes a totally different form and comes much closer to the truth. It's best to visit on a still, winter day. You have driven down the Tularosa Basin, with the snowcapped Sacramentos looming to your left and to your right, at the very bottom of the valley, mile after mile of the tortured black lava flow which New Mexicans call *malpais* (bad country). Now, far to the south, between you and the San Andres-Organ mountain chain, you see White Sands, a long white, shimmering line. Fifteen miles beyond the irrigated agricultural oasis of Alamogordo, Highway 70, angling southwestward toward its pass through the Organs, intersects with this whiteness. A National Park Service visitor's center, unmanned on this wintery evening, stands beside the highway. Past it, an access road leads westward over the alkali flats. And then the sands close around you. At the edges, some plants resist — saltbrush and iodine bush, skunkbush sumac, soap tree yucca and rubber pennyroyal — all species of incredible durability. But within moments, you inhabit a landscape of undulating white, surrounded by great dunes — some as high as thirty feet — of granulated gypsum crystals. You are in a landscape as dead and as pure as Antarctica.

There is nothing quite like it on the face of the earth. The name White Sands is misleading. This desert is not formed of sand. These dunes are born of water sweeping through the slopes of the surrounding mountains, eating away gypsum deposits and carrying this chemical in solution into the ten-mile long *playa* called Lake Lucero. Here the desert sun burns away the moisture, leaving sheets of dried gypsum crystals. These are eroded by the southwesterly wind. For hundreds of thousands of years this partnership of rain, sun and wind have moved the sands northeastward in a sheet which now covers 270 square miles.

When the air moves, the dunes march with infinite slowness. The crystals are carved out of their hard-packed southwestern slopes, pushed toward the soft summit, and rolled, finally, down the dune face a trillion-billion strong. They engulf the park service road and the skeleton of yucca, and whatever else lies in their path in an endless slow-motion surf.

By its nature, desert seems to resist the idea of time. Its leafless, spiny, sword-blade life ignores the cycle of seasons. Desert plants produce their brief explosion of flowers with more response to rare rainstorms than to any imagined seasonal fecundity. Spring brings only the arid wind and the dust devils hurrying aimlessly over a landscape of gray and brown and muted reds. (Over the White Sands, even these dust devils change. Instead of weightless dust, the spiralling winds pick up the heavy whiteness and hang almost motionless — glittering ropes connecting dunes and sky.) Within the Sands, this desert illusion of timelessness is intensified. On a windless winter afternoon here, the very planet seems dead. The silence is as pure as the crystals on which you stand. To the west, the Organs form an implausible ragged line against the sunset. To the northwest, the reflected light reddens the Sacramentos and highlights the snowpack on Sierra Blanca. The nearest fellow human is a long day's walk away.

Of course, there is more than this. There is the wind hooting through those odd volcanic walls which form miles-long rays from the base of the Shiprock. (A thousand feet overhead, among the crags of the monolith, Monster Slayer tricked the Winged Monster and killed it, and taught its offspring to be eagles. Thus was this area made safe for Navajos.) There is the old stone village of Zuni on Shalako night — playing host to the towering Messenger Birds and the Council of the Gods and feeding three thousand curious visitors on mutton stew and canned peaches. And Santa Fe under fresh snow — its ancient narrow streets looking like nothing else in America. And Aspen Basin when the leaves are falling from a thousand stark-white trunks — vertical lines that connect yellow floor with yellow ceiling. And the canyons of the Pajarito Plateau where you still find Keresan magic scratched into the stone.

New Mexico is all of this, and a great deal more.

New Mexico

New Mexico, Taos Pueblo, David Muench

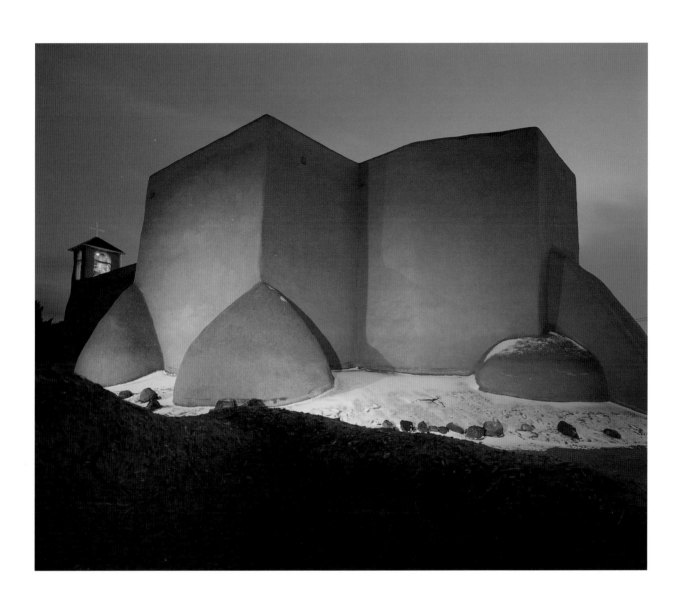

New Mexico, St. Francis Church in Rancho de Taos, David Muench

New Mexico, Yucca and Dunes, David Muench

New Mexico, White Sands National Monument, David Muench

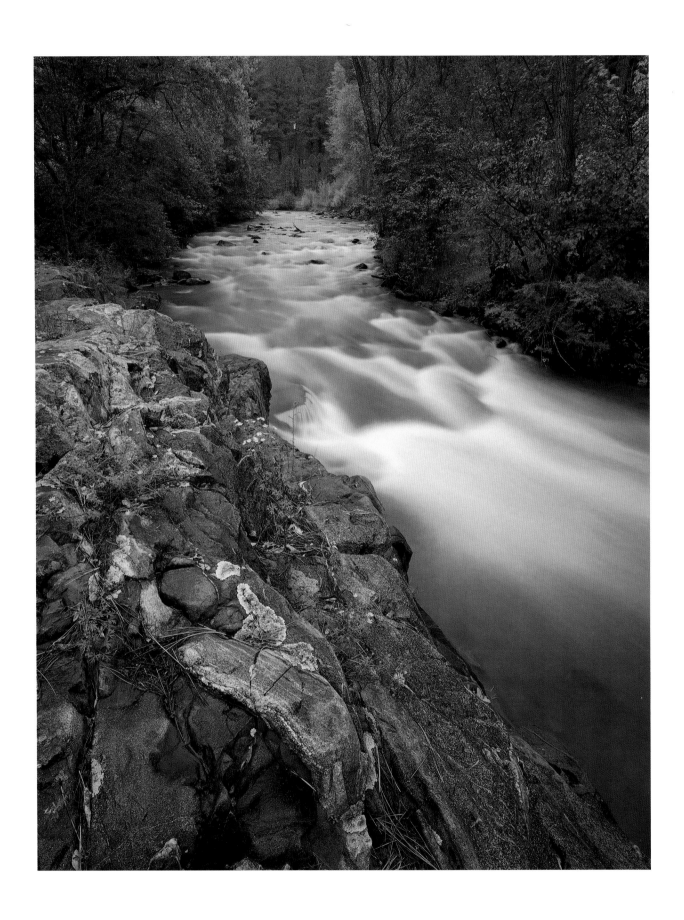

New Mexico, Pecos River, David Muench

New Mexico, Wheeler Park Wilderness, Marc Muench

New Mexico, Ship Rock, David Muench

New Mexico, Sacramento Mountains, David Muench

A Canyon, Chaco Canyon Kivas, David Muench

A Canyon, an Egret, and a Book

On page 185 of *A Thief of Time,* readers encounter a snowy egret, flushed from his roosting place in the San Juan River Canyon by a Navajo Tribal Policeman. The policeman is fictional. But the canyon is real and so is the startled egret, flying majestically away into the darkness down the canyon. Therein lies a tale of how a book evolved and how a silent, empty place can stimulate the human imagination.

It happened because of one of those odd confluences of needs which sometimes occurs. I needed locations, and inspiration, for a book that was trying to take shape in my head. Specifically I needed an Anasazi cliff dwelling in an isolated place. There I intended to have a pot hunter murder an anthropologist. That was to be the pivotal point in a story about those "thieves of time" who loot ancient ruins. Since the anthropologist, the pot hunter, and the crime would be pure fiction, it would seem logical that the cliff dwelling could be fictional as well. But logic doesn't apply when I am trying to write a book. For some reason I need to virtually memorize the landscapes I write about.

Meanwhile, two other coinciding needs had developed. Dan Murphy of the U.S. Park Service was feeling a need to show me — a skeptic — that the San Juan River canyon above Lake Powell was as awe-inspiring as he had been claiming. And Charles DeLorme of Wild River Expeditions at Bluff, Utah, needed two people to go along on a raft trip he was organizing. He needed someone to explain to his paying guests the geology, flora, and fauna of the canyon they would be seeing, and someone to tell them campfire stories about the mythology, culture, and history of the Navajos, through whose territory the river wanders. Thus Murphy and I signed on to float down the San Juan as natural historian and yarn spinner, respectively.

Wild Rivers Expeditions begins most of its San Juan float trips at Sand Island, downstream a bit from Bluff. Just west of the launch site, the river passes under the bridge carrying Highway 191 on its way to Mexican Water and the tiny Navajo settlement of Tes Nez Iah in Arizona. It meanders about for a time between gradually rising cliffs of sandstone, colored pale pink and salmon. Then the bluffs close in and the sandy banks narrow. About seven miles from the launch point, the river slashes through one of the nation's more spectacular geological features. Geologists call it the Monument Upwarp—a place where the earth's crust was thrust up in an immense bubble. The dome of this bubble eroded away millions of years ago but the base remains. On its long, relatively steep drop toward its junction with the Colorado River—a junction now drowned by Lake Powell—the San Juan zigzags its way through this geological oddity. First it flows through the Lime Ridge and Raplee anticlines, layered strata which slant sharply upward as the rafter passes older and older formations which elsewhere lie deeper and deeper under the earth's crust. Since the cliff walls are also rising around you, this slant gives the eerie sensation that the river is plunging toward the center of the planet. On the other side of this upwarp (the Mexican Hat Syncline) the strata slant the opposite way, reversing the effect. Now one seems to be floating rapidly uphill.

While this exposure of the planet's geologic secrets has its fascination, I was more interested in relatively recent history. The same Anasazi people who built great stone apartment towns in places like Mesa Verde and Chaco Canyon only to walk away from them had also appeared in small family groups in this stony wilderness. For my novel about a crime, I intended to use as characters the anthropologists who try to solve the secret of this vanished civilization. And as you float down the San Juan from Sand Island, Anasazi traces are quick to appear.

About three miles into this journey, we pulled our rafts onto the north shore and inspected an unexcavated mound where some nine hundred years of drifted dust buried an Anasazi ruin. Above it, footholds cut into the stone mark the path they used to reach the mesa top. A mile later, we made another stop and examined what is, in effect, an Anasazi mural. Here petroglyphs were cut through the dark manganese oxide ("desert varnish") stains on the sandstone face of the cliff—forming rows and rows of figures. Some I could identify. One was obviously a snowy egret. Others are abstract representations of the reptiles, birds, and animals which still inhabit the canyon (or, like the bighorn sheep, have vanished with the Anasazis). But many of the forms seem to be from the world of the spirit. Humanoid shapes with great square shoulders cut into the stone here represent (anthropologists believe) the kachina spirits which still play a central role in the metaphysics of the Pueblo tribes. On this cliff, stripes are cut over their heads indicating whatever one's imagination suggests—perhaps speech, or song, or rank among magicians.

My own imagination was trying to deal with this remarkable mural cliff through the eyes of two fictional characters. One is Lieutenant Joe Leaphorn of the Navajo Tribal Police, whom I've used for years and know as one knows a dear old friend. No problem with Joe. I know how his mind works. But the other character was a still nebulous stranger—my murder victim. I had decided to make this victim a contract archaeologist working for the U.S. Park Service at the Chaco Cultural Center in New Mexico. On this hot July afternoon on the river this character was a male, and existed only as about forty-five words on paper on my desk in Albuquerque. He was to be a specialist in something yet to be decided, and he was supposed to be dead by the end of the first chapter—the victim of the murder on which the plot of this book will turn.

As I stared at figures cut into this cliff, I found myself thinking of the artists who carved it. They would have used tools of sharpened antlers and flint. It would have been a hard, hot job on an summer day like this. I thought of their scarred and calloused hands. That led me to remember the hands of a woman archaeologist I know—a beautiful, graceful young woman with the desert sun complexion of the Southwest who rarely is seen without at least one finger bandaged. Suddenly I found myself thinking of my murder victim as a woman. She had the scarred, calloused hands of digging archaeologists and a Phi Beta Kappa mind. She was a working-class woman—an oddity in this field. Thus, under this cliff where Anasazi artists toiled a thousand years ago, what had been a disposable, one-dimensional character changed gender and developed a personality, with a memory of family, with a failed marriage, an admiration for an older man she wants to impress, and a love of the abstract art she sees on this cliff. It's a shame, I think, that she has to die so soon.

The water the San Juan carries is mostly high mountain snow melt. It emerges from the Navajo Dam in New Mexico crystal clear and an almost constant 42 degrees Fahrenheit. By the time it reaches here, it has been colored by sand and silt. But even in summer, it is still cold enough to give you a shock when your raft splashes through the river's modest rapids. Here the current flowing over the river's granular bottom creates a pattern of dunes much as prevailing winds form them in the desert. These in turn cause "sand waves." Our raft splashes along over these in a series of miniature roller coaster rides, countering the blistering afternoon sun with a cooling spray.

We have been floating past cliffs formed mostly of pale pink Navajo Sandstone streaked with dark brown stains of manganese oxide. Now, a little less than six miles down from Sand Island, Murphy showed us where the very top of the darker Kayenta formation is visible at water level on the left. Just ahead, also on the Navajo side of the river, the stone walls of a small Anasazi cliff dwelling are visible high under the arched roof of the wall of a small side canyon. We drifted past that canyon's mouth. On the opposite side of the river a massive sandstone overhang shelters another ruin—some of its walls still intact all the way to the natural stone roof. We pulled up on the sandbar to take a look.

The raft crew calls this place "River House." Its most prominent feature is a roundish stone tower which looks a little like a silo and must have been used for storage of grain or other foodstuff. Where the food came from is another matter. Now the vegetation consists of tamarisk, Russian olives and tumble weeds—all relatively modern European imports—and such ancient American plants as broom snakeweed, sagebrush, chamisa, prickly pear, yucca, box elder, seep willow, three wing saltbush, Indian rice grass, Spanish dagger, poison ivy, and a few cottonwoods. The river is the home of catfish, a few beaver, and muskrats. And I've seen antelope, ground squirrels, a gopher snake, and short-horned, collared, and desert spiny lizards. I have also spotted swallows, ravens, a red-tailed hawk, two turkey vultures, and a single American kestrel—not enough raptors to suggest that this stony canyon offers much meat to eat. But that's not my mystery. Mine was how to make this book take shape.

It was cool on the earthen floor of River House, and quiet—a good place to sit and think bookish thoughts. This ruin, like most along the San Juan drainage, has been surveyed and listed by the anthropological/archaeological establishment, but never officially excavated by a research team. However, it has been probed by pot hunters. They have left shallow holes in the hummock of earth which must have been this family's trash heap and is, therefore, a likely place for Anasazi burials. It has also been vandalized—one of its walls broken down and other damage done. The raft crew, from which the river has no secrets, told me the vandal is a member of an unpopular Navajo family which had moved across the river from the reservation. They described him as a boy with severe emotional problems.

And so, while I sat in River House looking at the damage this boy has done, a possible first chapter took shape. A Navajo boy, a neurotic loner, would be a witness to my intended murder. I convert him from a vandal per se into a would-be artist who paints his own pictographs on cliffs. My Navajo policeman sees them, knows by their nature that they must be of modern Navajo origin, finds the boy, solves the crime. But this River House is not an appropriate scene for my crime. Its site overlooking the San Juan is too visible. I need isolation. Besides, Murphy had told me there is a much better ruins downstream and up a canyon on the Navajo side of the river.

From River House, an old trail leads a half mile downstream to the mouth of Comb Wash and up the wash to traces of an old road which climbs Comb Ridge. The road was cut by the Mormons sent down from the Salt River Valley by Brigham Young to establish an outpost on the San Juan near where Bluff is now located. Comb Ridge is a barrier of solid rock, part of the great Monument Upwarp. Scouts for the Mormon wagon train must have ridden down the Wash for miles looking for a break in the wall. Finding none, they had decided to chip out a road over it. They were dealing with getting ox-drawn wagons over an abrupt vertical rise of at least four hundred feet—about the equivalent of a forty-story building—with nothing but hand tools, their own muscles, and faith in their God. For me it was an ordeal to huff and puff up the traces of that old exploit, burdened with nothing heavier than a canteen.

The road leads past a circular mound which must cover the remains of an unusually large ceremonial kiva. It offers an impressive long view over the Bluff Valley and the sandstone wilderness that surrounds it. The climb also produced thoughts about the sort of iron-willed men and women who were the ancestors of Bluff.

Thus, *A Thief of Time* took another of its quirky turns. I decided I would try to work in just such a Mormon as a character—an elderly man if possible. Not many months before, the home of a prominent citizen of this Southern Utah canyon country had been raided by the federals. The man's collection of artifacts had been seized and he'd been accused of dealing in illegal Anasazi pots. For my purposes, that was perfect material for the sort of red herring subplot I'm always needing.

Beside the river below this high edge of Comb Ridge, there still stands the stone foundation of a water wheel the settlers installed to grind their grain into flour. On the barren shelf of sandstone above this old mill, there's the roofless ruins of a one-room building. Murphy told me this structure was built as a trading post, that its owner was shot to death in a dispute with two Navajo customers—who then fled across the San Juan and vanished in the wilderness of erosion across the river. When we pushed off again from the sandbar at River House Ruins, that story, too, was stuck in my memory.

I found myself looking for a spot where two men—probably poor swimmers—could have crossed without drowning. Could my fictional neurotic young Navajo swim? Such bootless mental exercises explain why writers of fiction have reputations for blank expressions and absent-mindedness. This train of thought was occupying my imagination when our approaching raft caused the snowy egret to fly.

He rose out of a clump of tamarisk and seep willows on a sandbar just ahead of our raft, headed down-river. He flew slowly, no more than six feet above the water, a graceful shape gleaming white against the dark, shadowed cliffs ahead. And then he disappeared around a river bend. I remembered the petroglyph egret. A thousand years ago, I think, the Anasazi artist saw an identical bird and was impressed enough to preserve him in stone.

Since childhood I have been a person impressed by birds — an idle, amateur student of crow migrations, of how mocking birds tease cats, and blue jays dive-bomb them, of the kaleidoscope patterns that snow geese use to form their first dawn flights from water, of the concentrated patience of the heron waiting for the minnow to move nearer. Here was just one egret, no mate, no companions. Are snowy egrets, like swans and wolves, among those species that mate only once, and for life? What holds this great bird in such a lonely, empty place?

By the time we were rolling out our sleeping bags and building our evening fire at the mouth of Chinle Wash, several things were coming clear about the book. The egret would have his place in it somehow, and the thoughts his solitary presence had provoked seemed to be turning a tale of action I had intended into a novel of character. I found myself trying to attach the same perpetual monogamy I had imagined for the egret to one of the characters. I tried it first on the victim. (By now she has become Dr. Eleanor Friedman-Bernal to me, with the hyphenated Bernal to drop as soon as her divorce became final.) It didn't work. She is the wrong type. I turn from that to collecting the sort of impressions she would collect as she arrived at this place. She would make the trip secretively and at night since her dig would be illegal. She would be burdened with that sort of nervousness that law-abiding people feel when they are breaking the law. Still, she would be stirred by this evening as I am stirred. Violet-green swallows and "nighthawks" are out, patrolling the twilight for insects. I remember an argument I used to have with the Potawatomie boys I played with as a child about whether they should be called "bullbats" instead. A beaver, looking old and tired, swims slowly up the river, keeping out of the current and paying no more attention to me than he would to a cow. I hear the song of frogs coming from somewhere up the wash and, as the rising moon lights the tops of the cliff, a coyote and his partner begin exchanging coyote talk somewhere high above us on Nokaito Bench. The swallows and

A Canyon, an Egret, and a Book

nighthawks call it an evening and are replaced by battalions of bats. They flash through the firelight making their high-pitched little calls. I make notes of all of this, using reality to spare my imagination. I still had a lot of work to do on this plot.

One of those noisy and torrential thunderstorms which make summer interesting on the Colorado Plateau (Navajos call them "male rains") had swept across the Chinle Wash drainage fairly recently. While not a drop seemed to have fallen here at its junction with the San Juan, a substantial flash flood had roared down the wash. The bottom was muddy and the potholes still held water. In these, the eggs of leopard frogs had hatched and the new generation (about thumbnail size) was everywhere ahop. Such frogs are exactly the sort of specific details I look for, hoping they make fictional landscapes seem real. I would remember these frogs.

For a collector of such odds and ends as leopard frogs, Dan Murphy is a perfect guide. He had come to show me a specific cliff dwelling. But en route he showed me the trap door lid under which a wolf spider was lurking, the way a species of black, crumbly and dead-seeming desert lichen will turn a gaudy green when touched by water, a Navajo pictograph in which a man on foot is shooting an arrow at a big-hatted horseman who is shooting a pistol at him, fossils of crinoids, horn coral, and various brachiopods, and so forth. He also showed me "Baseball Man," an unusual Anasazi pictograph which depicts — larger than life — a figure which seems to be holding a big reddish chest protector, like a home plate umpire. But the cliff dwelling at the end of this long walk was the prize.

Reaching it involved climbing out of the wash bottom onto a broad stone shelf. This led to a second level of cliffs and past another of those petroglyph murals. This one was decorated with beautifully preserved depictions of the little humpbacked flute player which anthropologists call Kokopela (including one of him on his back, flute aimed between his knees.) Anthropologists believe Kokopela was the Anasazi fertility figure and one sees him carved into cliffs and painted on lava rocks throughout Anasazi country. At the moment I was thinking of his flute. Specifically I was considering how eerie it would seem if my foredoomed anthropologist, aware of the presence of these figures, hears the piping of his music in the canyon darkness. But how? Can I make my neurotic Navajo a musician? That seems strained. I dismissed the idea. It refused to go away.

The flute player notion was still with me when we reached the ruins Murphy had thought were exactly right for my purposes. They were far better than anything I could have imagined. Behind a curve in the towering sandstone wall of the mesa, nature had formed a cavernous amphitheater some fifty feet deep, sixty feet wide and perhaps seventy feet from floor to ceiling. A seep high up the face of the cliff produced enough water to cause a green curtain of moss and ivy to thrive beneath it and to feed a shallow basin perhaps ten or twelve feet across on the stone floor of the alcove. Behind this pool on a ledge some twelve feet above the alcove floor an Anasazi family had built its stone home. The centuries had done their damage but the walls of the small structure were mostly intact. Up the cliff at the edge of the alcove a stairway-ladder of footholds had been cut into the stone. They led to a shelf high above. There another stone structure stood. It must have been built as the family's desperate last defense if danger came and trapped them.

This high hideaway is unusual but the overhang itself is typical enough of the alcoves the Anasazis preferred as living sites. It faced so that it was open to the low winter sun, but protected from the summer sun almost overhead. Beyond the deep shade around the pool, blinding sunlight reflected off the sandy humps and the bare stone of the mesa. But it was cool here and silent — out of the reach of the breeze which was kicking up whirls of dust along Chinle Wash. The pool had produced its own swarm of the inevitable leopard frogs. Sitting there watching them provoked thoughts. Were those drought-resistant frogs here when the Anasazi family occupied the house behind me? How would it have felt to have lived in this lonely place at the tag end of a dying culture? What danger was so fierce that it caused these people to build their tiny little fort?

I imagine the family huddled behind the walls above. I make it night. A dark night. Something has frightened them into scurrying up the footholds. They hold their breath, listening. Hearing what? The Anasazis become Eleanor Friedman-Bernal, already uneasy by the illegality of her dig here, and now hiding, terrified. What does she hear? I think of Kokopela's flute — music from a spirit vanished a thousand years. Crazy, I think. And while I am into the craziness, I try again to do something with the neurotic Navajo. I change him to a neurotic local Mormon boy. A boy whose only relief from some mental illness is music. But what is he doing here? Hiding out from some crime I will dream up later. What else would Eleanor hear? The frogs, perhaps. The frogs are hopping about on the fringes of the pool. I try to look at the frogs through the eyes of the mentally ill boy I have hiding here. The majestic snowy egret reinserts itself into this daydreaming, and with it my speculation about its loneliness and its faithfulness. An idea comes, and another.

Gradually, as I sit in that cool shade among the frogs my Navajo Tribal policeman became a widower, and the framework for my tale became the makings of a novel.

It took another trip down the San Juan Canyon, and up Chinle Wash, before I could complete it all. This time I went during what the Navajos call "the Season when the Thunder Sleeps." In this rainless time, the potholes in the wash were dry, and so was the pool under the ruins. The frogs had vanished, leaving their eggs waiting in the dried mud for a wetter time. The snowy egret had vanished, too. But the ruins of the trading post on the shelf above the river were there, and I visited them again because now they were sticking in my mind. How could a crime that had destroyed a family a generation ago leave a memory that would destroy a man today? I began to see how it could happen.

And thus the San Juan Canyon, already alive with its own old myths and mysteries, germinated another story.

A Canyon, Kiva, Robert Reynolds

A Canyon, Tuft Trail in Bandelier, Robert Reynolds

A Canyon, Gila Cliff Dwellings, David Muench

A Canyon, Petroglyphs, David Muench

A Canyon, Spanish Dagger, Robert Reynolds

A Canyon, Egret, Robert Reynolds

A Canyon, Puye Cliff Dwelling, Robert Reynolds

Rio Grande, Colorado Canyon, David Muench

Rio Grande

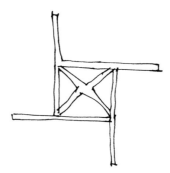

It begins at the Continental Divide, on the backbone of North America, and its nineteen-hundred-mile journey to the Gulf of Mexico makes it second only to the Missouri-Mississippi in length among the continent's rivers. It drains a quarter-million square miles of the Southern Rockies, the Southwest, and Mexico. Yet in certain places and in certain seasons one can walk across its bed and get nothing on his shoes but dust. Of all the world's great rivers only the water of the Ganges is more heavily used to irrigate crops. Yet in 1970 Congress made it the first stream officially named a "Wild River" to preserve its still untouched canyons for those who love the wilderness.

At places it is a clear, cold trout stream. At others it is grey with silt, or orange with the mud from the Rio Chama, drained dry by irrigation diversion, or green with explosive growth of algae and other water plants. We call it the Rio Grande, but on Mexican maps it is the Rio Bravo. It has had at least a dozen other names. Alonso Alvarez de Piñeda sailed his galleon into its mouth in 1519 and called it Rio de las Palmas in recognition of the jungle of palm trees that covered its delta. The scouts of Don Juan de Oñate found it a thousand miles upstream in 1598 when the May floods were roaring down from the mountains. After it drowned two of their horses, they named it Rio Bravo del Norte—the Wild River of the North. A sailor shipwrecked from the fleet of Francis Drake crossed it in what is now south Texas and, charmed by its serene lushness, called it the River of May. I have lived along it much of my life, studied it, fished it, washed in it, floated down it, and it seems to me that no American river can match the richness of its history, its variety, or its power to stir the imagination.

The source of the Rio Grande is a high, horseshoe valley just under Stony and Humpback passes in the San Juan Mountains of southern Colorado. I was last here on September 21—the last day of summer and the beginning of fall. But at almost two and a half miles above sea level the few days that pass for summer are far behind and there's not much left of autumn. Behind me Pole Mountain rises to 13,740 feet. To the northeast Bent, Cuba, and Carson Peaks—all well over 13,000—form the horizon. The south is walled off by the Rio Grande Pyramids, which reach to almost 14,000 feet. To the west stand Canby, Hunchback, and Nebo Peaks, connected by saddleback passes. Inside this sky-high enclosure is an irregular grassy depression, more than ten miles across. Its upper margins are the broken grey of talus slopes, spotted and streaked with the white of snowpacks, which summer is never quite long enough to melt. (If you dig deep enough through the hard, late-summer snow, you encounter blue-white ice left over, perhaps, from the Age of Glaciers.) But most of the immense bowl is the muted green of the life zone biologists call arctic-alpine. Here grow the quick seeding sedges, the short, tough tundra grasses, and—along the streams—the squat, durable bushes and the reeds and tuberous plants that flourish in the dank soil where cold water seeps. Here, no plant grows that cannot survive high winds, 60-below-zero Fahrenheit temperatures and the crushing burden of compacted snow.

The world here is too harsh for most mammals. Even the snowshoe rabbit and the ubiquitous chipmunk tend to stick to the protection of timberline far below. The sheep driven up the old Rocky Pass trail after the spring thaws are driven out again before the first heavy snows. One sees few birds. Now and then a golden eagle will drift overhead, but he's headed for better hunting down the slopes. An occasional Clark's nutcracker, pine grosbeak or rosy finch has staked out temporary feeding territory among the brushy places. But the only live thing which seems comfortable at home here is the pika. They move among the boulders like animated balls of brown fur, their whistling calls loud in the silence.

But even when the breeze (and the pikas) are still, the silence here is not quite absolute. There is always the sound of water. The water is everywhere. It dribbles down from hundreds of springs and seeps to feed scores of little brooks, which combine to become

Bear Creek, Pole Creek, and Middle Pole, and West Pole, and Quartzite, and the myriad arms of Deep Creek and, finally, where Deep and Pole merge under Timber Hill, the Rio Grande itself. Even when the heavy snows of autumn bury these streams, the muted sound of water-over-stone can still be heard. The modern record for snowfall on the Rio Grande watershed was set in the winter of 1951-1952, when an estimated fifty-five feet (enough to bury a five-story building) fell on Wolf Creek Pass. When measured on April 1, the snowpack, despite evaporation loss, melt, and the winter-long compression under its own crushing weight, was still 131 inches deep. It contained 55.3 inches of water, and the average Rocky Mountain snowfall contains one inch of water for one foot of snowfall.

It's difficult on a sunny autumn day to imagine Stony Pass basin buried under such an immensity of snow. It's even harder to visualize how different this valley will be when spring arrives and the high country begins to release this wealth of water. Every slope and hillside will be shiny then with the wetness of melting snow. The brooks that now barely trickle will be gushing. The network of creeks will flood with murky runoff. The faint music made by the exhausted streams of autumn will be replaced by the roar of cataracts.

The runoff season extends from early spring in the foothills to midsummer in the highest of the high country—but the heavy snowmelt period is usually compressed into a period of about forty days. In that span, after an average year of snowfall, an incredible five hundred million tons of water comes thundering down the mountain tributaries into the main stream of the Great River. After a wet winter, runoff sometimes exceeds a billion tons.

Before this runoff was checked, the Rio Grande in spring deserved the title "Rio Bravo." Its floods were wild indeed, making investment in irrigation works a risky business and the life expectancy of bridges short. A group of San Luis Valley farmers joined forces shortly before World War I to apply the first curb. Using mule power and packed-in supplies, they built the towering pile of earth that blocks the narrow slot between Finger Mesa and Simpson Mountain. On this quiet autumn day, the reservoir behind Farmer's Union Dam has been drained almost empty. The river snakes for miles through a bottom flattened by sixty years of silting, greened now by a quick growth of algae. From the dirt road that hugs the slope above it, the Rio Grande here looks like a silver snake on a billiard table. But by early next summer, this narrow valley will be filled with fifty thousand acre-feet of water in a lake eight miles long.

When it leaves this dam, the Rio Grande has traveled only a dozen miles from its origins. But it has already dropped more than three thousand feet to the 9,350-foot level — squandering 20 per cent of the altitude it will use to carry it halfway across America. The Rio Grande here is every man's dream of what a mountain river should be. And thus it remains for fifty miles. It runs over a clean bottom of gravel and polished boulders. It is cold, clear, rich in oxygen and alive with rainbow trout — a stream of rapids and deep pools and driftwood on its banks for fires to warm the fly-fishermen. It is hemmed in by mountains, with the La Garita Wild Area to the north and the San Juan Primitive Area to the south. The treeless tundra of the arctic-alpine zone is now far behind. The river has dropped quickly through the Hudsonian life zone — at this latitude a narrow belt of "wind timber" (stunted fir, Englemann spruce, white-barked pine and mountain hemlock). It has dropped past Shotgun Mountain into the great Upland Meadow, where for the first time its water is diverted to irrigate an expanse of hay fields. It circles the lonely eminence of Bristol Head Mountain and runs — for the only time in its long journey — almost due north toward Creede — the last of the boom silver towns, which crowds the narrow canyon of Willow Creek.

Creede is the capital and metropolis of the upper river — a village for which the map claims 350 residents. Its little schoolhouse serves a few-score children scattered through an area not much smaller than Connecticut. In the summer it is busy with fishermen and tourists. Now it is quiet, bracing for winter. Woodpiles tower beside houses, and in the Snowshoe Cafe the talk is of the brown bear that has been raiding garbage cans — fattening himself for hibernation.

Eight miles below Creede, the river pours through Wagon Wheel Gap. Reinforced by the waters of Goose Creek, South Fork, and Embargo Creek, it flows out into one of America's great intermountain parks—the San Luis Valley. Here the landscape, and the river, change drastically. Left behind now are the cool, dim forests of fir, spruce, and aspen. Now, away from the river, the flora is that of the cool, semi-arid climate of the Colorado Plateau. There is rabbit brush, chamisa, sage, silvery clumps of buffalo grass and the waving yellow cycles of grama grass. Then, as the valley opens, there are two-thirds of a million acres of farmland made fertile by the river itself.

This the first of the rich valleys through which the Rio Grande wanders. Most of them, like the river itself, are the product of a phenomenon of mind-boggling immensity. In terms of geological time it happened only yesterday—when many of America's other rivers had already been wearing away at their valleys for millions of years. Scientists can't time it exactly, but it came in the most recent era of the earth's formation—the Cenozoic—and in the age the geologists call the Miocene. The last of the dinosaurs had been extinct perhaps a hundred million years and the dominant life form of the continent was the mammal. We know only that twenty million years ago the Rio Grande didn't exist. About fifteen million years ago it did. In that interim, the continental midlands underwent dramatic changes.

Here, a section of the earth's crust about eight thousand square miles in area began sinking. At the same time, the crust around it rose, forming the San Juan and Sangre de Cristo mountains. The process was extremely slow but the results were impressive. An area a little larger than New Jersey was left as much as two miles lower than the land surrounding it. In the Albuquerque area, where this process still hasn't completely stabilized, the Sandia Mountains offer spectacular proof of the extent of this movement. To find the same strata of rocks that rims Sandia Crest almost eleven thousand feet above sea level, one has to drill a little more than sixty-five hundred feet below the bed of the Rio Grande that runs past the foot of the mountain. Thus in central New Mexico we know the vertical shift was more than two miles. In some places along the Rio Grande "graben" the gap is more than three miles.

At first these depressions were not connected. The mountains drained into them, forming huge inland seas. But time and gravity did their inevitable work. Millions of years of earthquakes, water erosion, glaciation and volcanic action gradually filled these lakes with stone, silt and ashes. The lake that once covered the San Luis Valley finally spilled over the great dam of volcanic basalt that had closed its southern end. It began cutting a channel, draining itself into the lake that covered the Española Valley below, causing it to overflow in turn. Thus the Rio Grande was born. Geologists believe the Rio Grande is a veritable infant among the continent's rivers — finally integrated to reach the Gulf of Mexico as late as five hundred thousand years ago.

At Alamosa on an autumn evening all this cosmic violence is hard to credit. Here alluvial fans have forced the river eastward, the towering San Juans have receded to a ragged line on the western horizon, and the Sangre de Cristos loom to the east. They are thirty miles distant, but in the luminous transparency of high, dry air they seem an easy walk away. A landscape as flat as Kansas wheat country stretches away in all directions. On this particular evening students from Adams State College are holding a picnic in the riverside park just inside the grassy old levee that protects the town from floods. Below the levee the river lies in long, still pools. The water seems dead, but the yellow leaves from the cottonwoods move on its surface — drawn inexorably southward. Between the voices of the students, there is the slightest suggestion of the music moving water makes. A family of muskrats make their home somewhere along this levee and one of them now swims slowly upstream on some chore — undismayed by collegiate laughter and my curiosity. Civilization has tamed him, as irrigation has tamed the river.

The first irrigation in the Upland Meadow does nothing more than water a few hundred acres, hardly affecting the stream. In the San Luis Valley, it's another matter. As the river reaches its junction with South Fork at the head of the valley, more than fifteen hundred cubic feet per second of its water is diverted into the big Del Norte ditch. Before it reaches Lobatos Bridge at the bottom of the valley, the river feeds seventy other ditches. These arteries serve a sprawling network of capillaries that carry the Rio Grande miles from its bed to reach almost seven hundred thousand otherwise arid acres. Before the Del Norte Ditch was built in 1882, the San Luis Valley was too dry to raise much more than cattle, hay and a few chancy crops of grain when it was unusually rainy. Now it produces an annual wealth of potatoes, sugar beets, cereals and vegetables. In its wandering, 150-mile course throughout the valley, Rio Grande water is used again, and again, and again. The seepage from croplands is collected in drains, returned to the river, and diverted again to repeat the process. By the time it reaches the Colorado-New Mexico border, it is a tired, depleted river. But here it begins new life and takes on a new character.

The San Luis Valley had been home only for nomadic Indians. The Stone Age hunters of the last Ice Age had come and gone. And then, thousands of years later, bands of Athabascan Indians moved into the park looking for the homeland they would call Dinetah and their destiny as the Navajo Nation. They were driven southward by fiercer people, Sioux and Cheyenne encroaching from the north, Comanches from the eastern Buffalo Plains, and the Utes. The first recorded white expedition into the vast valley was drawn there in a counterattack against these raiders. A pugnacious Comanche war chief named Greenhorn (in recognition of the green buffalo horn on his invincible helmet) was operating out of the valley to raid Indian pueblos and Spanish settlements downriver. Governor Juan de Anza of the Territory of New Mexico organized a mixed Spanish-Indian army of six hundred men. He pursued the Comanches up the valley and over Poncha Pass. Greenhorn donned his magic helmet and was killed with a dozen of his warriors in the ensuing cavalry skirmish. The expedition told the Spanish that the source of the Rio Grande was the San Juan Mountains (and not somewhere near the North Pole as some had suspected) and left the immense valley of its source open for settlement.

But the Spanish already had more land and Indian trouble in New Mexico than they could handle. Except for a few brave souls who moved into the lower end of the valley in the nineteenth century, white settlement generally waited until the end of the Civil War brought rapid western expansion of the United States. It wasn't until 1868 that the United States officially took the valley away from the Utes, opening it for homesteading and giving the tribe title to a perpetual reservation in the San Juan Mountains, which no one at the moment wanted. However, eternity proved brief for the Utes. Two years after the treaty was signed, prospectors searching for gold in violation of the agreement found a rich lode across Stony Pass. Miners poured in to develop the Silverton lode, the Stony Pass road was built to supply Silverton, and in 1873 the Utes were handed an amendment to their treaty in which they surrendered their rights to the San Juans. (Tribal survivors today are reduced to an arid, overgrazed patch of land in extreme southwestern Colorado.)

If you stand on the worn plank floor of the Lobatos Bridge just north of the New Mexico border, the only visible reminders of the tribes that once controlled the valley to the north are their sacred mountains. To the west, overlooking the Conejos River, is the cinder cone the maps call Ute Mountain, where the shamans of the tribe communed with their God. Directly upriver to the north looms Mount Blanca, one of the six sacred mountains of Navajo mythology. The Navajos call it *Naajini* (White Shell Mountain). It was built by First Man and First Woman, who spread a blanket of white shell on the earth and piled upon it soil carried up from the dim, subterranean Third World. On top of this, more white shell was spread, and Dawn Boy, one of the Holy People of the Navajos, entered the mountain to guard Dinetah (the Land of the People) from the east. Dawn Boy still lives there, watched over forever by Shash, the magic bear. But the people he was to guard are gone. The Rio Grande must pour through its great lava gorge into the Española Valley before it finds Indians who make it a part of their mythology and float the spirits of their dead upon its waters.

The line between the Rio Grande of the San Luis Valley and the Rio Grande below is appropriately abrupt and dramatic. It is formed by the Taos Plateau — a layer of volcanic basalt and ash up to a quarter mile deep through which the river has sliced the great zigzag canyon called the Rio Grande Gorge.

Lobatos Bridge is at the very end of the San Luis. The flat croplands are gone now, and the land beside the river rises in gentle mounds — the time-worn flanks of old, and minor, volcanic eruptions. It isn't flat enough here to irrigate, and it's too dry for trees — a sagebrush climate. The river lies in long, almost motionless pools in a shallow, gently sloping valley. The canyon develops a caprock rim only a few hundred yards above the bridge. As far as you can see downstream, this rim rises no more than fifty feet. But this is the beginning. At this lonely bridge, that brotherhood which finds its thrills testing courage and skill against stone and fast water begins one of America's most challenging runs.

The American River Touring Association rates rivers on a scale similar to that used by mountain climbers to classify peaks and cliffs. The scale runs from an easy I to VI. The first twenty-four miles below Lobatos—from the bridge to Lee's Trail—is rated II. That means one with a rubber raft and "intermediate" experience can safely run it. Beyond Lee's Trail, the river becomes Class VI, which translates to "utmost difficulty—near limit of navigability"— a stretch of water that should be attempted only by a team of experts taking every precaution. Michael Jenkinson, author of *Wild River of America,* calls the stretch between Lee's Trail and the point where the Red River pours into the Rio Grande "pure nightmare." In that scant twelve miles, the river squanders 650 feet of its altitude. It's a thunderous passage, even at low water, with the river roaring through a convoluted series of chutes and rapids, breaking into plumes of spray on house-sized boulders, and slamming into the slick, blank wall of its canyon. Experts have made it through this slot in low-water seasons. But a team of professional river guides who tried it in the spring of 1970 gave up and climbed out after covering less than five miles in four dangerous and exhausting days. In relation to the vast sweep of geologic history, the gorge is new, formed in the last half million years—the last tick of cosmic time. The river cut through this fifty-mile volcanic block like a hot wire sinking into a cake of ice, and not enough centuries have passed for wind, rain and gravity to soften the effect. The walls are sheer, the canyon narrow, and at places it is almost a thousand feet from rim to river.

For one approaching the Rio Grande across the Sunshine Valley north of Taos, this phenomenon can produce an eerie effect. Nothing on this plateau suggests the nearness of a river. Sagebrush, chamisa, and grama grass stretch unbroken toward the western horizon. But as you near the rim of the still-invisible gorge, you become aware of a sound. You seem to hear it through the soles of your feet—a muted subterranean thunder as if Mother Earth herself were murmuring in her eternal sleep. The sound, of course, is the booming of cataracts—tons of water pounding over basalt boulders.

Down among those water-slick boulders there is no surcease from sound. From Lee's Trail, about a dozen miles south of the Colorado border, to the confluence of the Red River, the Rio is a bedlam of boiling rapids. The fishermen who are lured into this noisy world can reach the upper end of this strip with a 220-foot descent from the rim. Twelve miles downstream at the La Junta campground, it takes a vertical climb of more than eight hundred feet to reach earth's surface again. The trail is good, zigzagging safely up the cliff. But, safe or not, the effect is much like getting to the eightieth floor of a skyscraper without using the elevator.

Among a small fraternity of fiercely ardent New Mexico and Colorado trout fishermen, this sunken piece of river is known as "The Box." The pools they prefer are reached neither by Lee's nor La Junta trails. There are other ways down, rough and chancy, by which those agile, strong-lunged, brave and fanatic enough can lower themselves by dawn's light to a favorite pool and escape from the depth at sundown. The reward for this is a chance to catch German brown trout of trophy size (this piece of river is often called the best brown trout fishing in America), lunker rainbows, and— odd as it sounds—northern pike. The pike have appeared only recently. It's speculated that they made their way downstream from some Colorado lake and reproduced in the cold, oxygen-rich water of the deep canyon.

There is another reward not measurable in pounds and inches. A day spent at the bottom is a day spent in a world which has nothing to do with civilization. The sun reaches the river only as it passes overhead at midday. The cliffs cut off everything, making the horizon a thin strip of blue overhead. The thunder of water echoes from the basalt walls and engulfs you. With all this, there is the spicing of risk. The Rio Grande here demands respect. When the current is up, losing your footing on spray-slick stone can be lethal. Even a sprained ankle requires a complicated and time-consuming team rescue effort. I recall four such rescue missions in the past five years (a drowned rafter, a dead fisherman, and two who survived). In a society which has slain all its dragons, this noisy stretch of water serves a sort of primal purpose. The angler who emerges on the rim at sunset with the voice of the river shouting far below him tends to feel he has tested more than his fishing skill.

Below the mouth of Red River the Rio Grande briefly slows its pace. For the next ten miles the rapids rate only a Class III (challenging for those with intermediate experience). But at John Dunn Bridge, things change again. The bridge is the only water-level access to the river for vehicles in sixty-five miles from Lobatos to Taos Junction. A road follows the Rio Hondo canyon from the village of Arroyo Hondo to the river and then climbs the cliff on the west side via awesome switchbacks. If rafters don't leave the river here, they experience seventeen miles of the loneliest and wildest water anywhere. The stretch is rated Class V (exceptionally difficult for experts) and its Powerline Rapids, where rockslides divert the river against its wall, are called by Jenkinson "one of the toughest navigable rapids on this or any other river." On this lonely stretch the only signs a rafter will see that the planet is inhabited are the bottom of the Rio Grande Gorge Bridge (a structure so far overhead that it seems unreal) and the high-voltage cable which gives the rapids its name.

U.S. 64 crosses the river on the high bridge at the midpoint of the seventeen miles of wild water. Here, too, the lay of the sagebrush prairie makes the river invisible until the last moment. One second you are driving across a brushy flat; the next, the road-side has disappeared—and you, car, and highway are airborne. The span, supported on two pylons anchored on shoulders of the cliffs, soars two thousand feet across the gorge and eight hundred above the river—it's the nation's second-highest bridge. Here, air moving through the steel structure close at hand blends with the noise of water far below, forming a duet of wind and river. It's one of few places I know of where one has a reasonable chance of looking down on the flight of a golden eagle. These great predator birds nest in the canyon walls and hunt rodents along the cliffs. Snowy egrets and great blue herons also sometimes live in the canyon, and the mud cliff dwellings of swallows are everywhere on the lichen-stained canyon walls.

For the obvious reason that it offers the only water available for miles, less perpendicular portions of the gorge serve as a magnet for wildlife, including animals as large as mule deer and prong-horn antelope. Muskrats are plentiful, along with a few beaver, and the usual coyotes and bobcats there to prey on the small rodents.

At Lee's Trail one can also witness the improbable sight of Hereford cattle in various stages of the laborious process of getting a drink of water. Some are at the canyon bottom, resting for the long ascent, some are making their way nervously down the narrow switchback path from the west rim, some are on the return trip, catching their breath at the elbows of zigzag turns. Since it is clearly impossible for two of the animals to pass at most places on the trail without tumbling one off the cliff, the Herefords have worked out a protocol for this daily ordeal. They rest only at wide places and begin ascents and descents in groups, thereby reducing the odds of confrontations.

The gorge ends fifty miles south of the Colorado border at the place where Taos Creek, a tiny clear stream at the bottom of an incredible canyon, trickles into the river. At this point, the river bottom widens into waterside benches, the cliffs are lower, and the Rio Grande undergoes another of its changes of character. By now there is more water. Costilla Creek has made its small donation just south of the New Mexico border, Rio Hondo and Red River have added their more considerable waters, and a series of springs deep in the gorge have made substantial contributions. The largest of these, Big Arsenic, pours fifty-four hundred gallons per minute of pure, icy water out of a rockslide just upstream from La Junta trail. Thus revived, the Rio Grande enters its most historic territory — the Española Valley.

Ever since it emerged through Wagon Wheel Gap, the river has been running through a land dotted with Spanish names: San Luis, Del Norte, Antonito, Lobatos, Conejos, Alamosa. But these are nineteenth-century places — settlements that in this river's span of history date back to only yesterday. Civilization in the middle valleys of the Rio Grande is immensely older.

Scientists believe that man first saw the Great River more than twenty thousand years ago. The river was much larger then, carrying the meltwater of the last glaciers and the runoff from the pluvial rains. In this cooler, wetter valley the Stone Age hunters we call Clovis and Folsom Man preyed on now-extinct longhorn bison, giant ground sloth, and the tiny camel and horses of that era. Perhaps six thousand years ago, the climate along the river became much warmer and drier. Hunting — always a risky and marginal way of life—became impractical. Those who survived shifted from a meat to a vegetable economy—subsisting on nuts, berries and what they could dig from the ground. Then, perhaps two thousand years ago, corn appeared in the Rio Grande Valley.

Exactly where it came from, no one knows. Some of those whose civilizations flourished because of it have passed down the word of its origins in their myths. It was given them as a blessing from the gods. Among the Keresan-speaking Pueblos along the river, corn was the final gift to them from Latik, the Mother of All, who helped them emerge from the underworld, and who, before she left them, gave her people her heart, which was seed corn, and taught the tribal *caciques* the rules of life. Modern agronomists have sought in vain an explanation more scientific than this. Corn is a form of grass, but because of the way its seeds are tightly secured on a cob, it won't reproduce without the help of human cultivation. Therefore it could not, so it seems, evolve naturally.

However it evolved, corn made a food surplus, a sedentary agricultural life, and civilization possible along middle valleys of the great river. The first known communal settlement was about A.D. 250, at the Artificial Lake Site near what is now downtown Albuquerque. As early as A.D. 600, the art of pottery-making was widespread and the people who were to become the Pueblo Indians were developing a sophisticated social community and a complex architecture. By the year 1,000, when Europeans were suffering through the bloody savagery we call the Dark Ages, these people had flowered into one of the most humane, peaceful, and demo-cratic societies the world has ever known. This Golden Age of the Pueblos produced the great communal dwellings of Mesa Verde, Chaco Canyon, Frijoles Canyon, and elsewhere—some abandoned during an epic cycle of drought in the twelfth century, and some abandoned for reasons which remain a total mystery. Whatever the cause, the people moved away from the cliffs and plateaus closer to the Rio Grande, which they called *T'sina,* or *Kanyapakwa,* or *P'osoge*—depending on whether their language was Tewa, or Towa, or Keresan. (Whatever the language, the name translates to something close to "great river.") They included it in the mythology of their wanderings, and built diversion dams of stone where its banks were low, and chopped out ditches to lead its water into their fields of corn, beans and squash. And when Europeans finally came to this part of the Rio Grande, they found more than sixty of these peaceful little city-states flourishing in the middle valley.

It has been said before that the Pueblo civilization was fortunate that the Europeans were not the English — who with a stolid lack of malice would soon be exterminating the woodland tribes along the Eastern seaboard. They were also fortunate that the Spanish came late. The mouth of the river had been discovered by Piñeda's little fleet in 1519. Cortez was in the Valley of Mexico prior to that year fighting Aztecs, and the brothers Pizarro were still thirteen years away from their conquest of Peru. But almost eighty years passed before the Spanish finally found time to convert the discovery into colonization — and in those eighty years history worked in complicated ways. The river was destined to see a different generation of conquistadores. The climate of the times had changed and with it some of the fierce, cruel, self-confident arrogance had mellowed out of the cutting edge of the Spanish empire. When the Spanish finally came to the middle river to stay, the moody, deeply religious Philip II had replaced Charles V on the throne of Spain. Pope Leo X had died. The Catholic theologians had declared that the natives of the New World were humans, exactly as the Spanish. The Indians were the sons of God. The Good News of Christianity must be preached to them so that they might become beloved subjects of the Two Majesties — the cross and the crown. Instead of Cortez, the gentle Pueblo cities received Don Juan de Oñate — and survived with their culture intact.

But it was a narrow escape.

Piñeda had been impressed with what he had seen at the mouth of this river — a flat, mild land forested with coconut palms. The river was muddy but deep, meandering through a vast delta. The people were uncivilized and poor, with no sign of agriculture. But they were friendly enough, providing the Spanish with shellfish, nuts, and berries in exchange for cloth and bells. The river must lead toward the Pacific Ocean, which Balboa had discovered just six years before. Piñeda called it the River of Palms and recommended to his *jefe*, Governor Garay of Jamaica, that a settlement be founded without delay. The following year, Diego de Camargo arrived with a small fleet to establish a town in Garay's name. He picked a site upstream from what is now Port Isabel, began building a fort, alienated the Indians, and escaped to sea after a wild ship-versus-canoe battle down twenty miles of river. In 1522, Garay himself came with a stronger force, but changed his mind and decided, instead, to contest Cortez for control of the Panuco River territory to the south. That ended Garay. Next, the notorious Nuño de Guzmán and Panfilo de Narváez were both given jurisdiction over the Rio Grande in overlapping grants from the Crown. Guzmán's plans for a colony came to nothing. Narváez, who also planned a settlement, produced instead a spectacular, epic disaster which would finally affect the Pueblos—one thousand miles upstream.

Narváez, faced with storms in the Gulf, landed his expedition on the west coast of Florida and sent his fleet westward. But the ships were lost, and the army disintegrated. Only five men are known to have survived of the four hundred landed. Four of them reached Mexico City in 1536 after seven years and some three thousand miles of wandering. They had reached the Rio Grande at about the present site of El Paso. The Indians there lived in dug-outs and thatched huts and were poor to the point of starvation. The four wanderers had lived with them for months, and listened to stories of a rich civilization up the river where the Indians lived in multistoried cities and used gemstones for arrowheads. One of the survivors was Nuñez Cabeza de Vaca, Royal Treasurer of the Narváez colony and a man to be believed. Among ambitious men in Mexico City, the tales of Cabeza de Vaca spread and grew. In 1539, Francisco Vásquez de Coronado sent another of the survivors—a Negro named Estebanico—and a Franciscan priest named Friar Marcus de Niza to explore. Estebanico was killed at one of the Zuni pueblos, but Friar Marcus returned and reported what he had seen and heard. He had seen villages of puddled adobe, and fields of corn, and a terraced town of stone, but he had heard of Cíbola, which the Indians told him consisted of seven cities—their streets paved with turquoise and their people decorated with golden ornaments. In 1540, twenty-one years after Piñeda's discovery, Coronado launched his famous expedition to find Cíbola and find out what lay up the Great River of the North.

It might be said that Coronado fell somewhere between Oñate and Cortez in nature as well as historic time. He took the

Zuni pueblos by storm, killing twenty warriors, but treated the survivors humanely. When the pueblos the Spanish called Arenal and Moho revolted, Arenal and most of its defenders were burned. But during the fifty-day siege of Moho, Coronado arranged the safe evacuation of women and children when the pueblo's water supply was exhausted. And when the defense finally collapsed, the Indian wounded received medical care and the prisoners were released. Coronado was an explorer, not a settler. He probed a thousand miles into the buffalo plains seeking the illusion of Quivira, a sort of golden Oz of the grass country. His lieutenants probed up the river as far as Taos Pueblo and down the river to the vicinity of El Paso. (There in late summer they saw one of the characteristics of the Rio Grande which still surprises Easterners. They reported the river vanished under its sandy bed, only to surface again far downstream.) In 1542, Coronado withdrew his army from the river and went home to Mexico to die. His expensive failure thoroughly disillusioned the Spanish, and the river flowed in peace for another forty years.

The great and fundamental change began for the middle valley in 1598. On April 20, Don Juan de Oñate arrived at the River of the North, and with him came 130 families, 270 soldiers, 11 Franciscan priests, and 7,000 head of livestock. Oñate was to be royal governor of a new colony and extend effective control by the Spanish Empire almost a thousand miles northward. The people with him came to stay, and stay they did. After almost four hundred years their family names are still the place names of the river country.

Oñate had reached the river several miles downstream from the present site of El Paso. He had abandoned the old, roundabout route to the Rio Grande, which followed up the valley of the Rio Conchos to Junta de los Rios, and explored a shorter and more direct passage. His route became known as the Camino Real, the Royal Road that would for two and a half centuries be the only artery connecting Mexico City with the river colony. While shorter, it was still a hideously difficult two-thousand-mile trek across the deserts. For two hundred fifty years, the Rio Grande colony would suffer from the extreme isolation from military and economic support.

Before he moved his party upriver, Oñate celebrated his arrival with a solemn High Mass at an altar under the cottonwoods, and a fiesta at which a play was presented. It dramatized the conversion of the Indians to Christianity by the Franciscan friars. It was a prophetic performance. By September, with his capital established across the river from the pueblo he named San Juan, Oñate invited leaders of all pueblos to a meeting. Thirty-two were represented at the session. The *caciques* were asked first to swear allegiance to the new government. They agreed to do so. They were then told of Christianity by Friar Alonzo Martínez, one of the Franciscans, and asked to accept the new faith. After a discussion among themselves the Indian spokesman said they would like to learn about it, but the bargain would be that they would become Christians only if they liked what they were taught. And so it started. Each of the priests was assigned to a group of Pueblos, and departed alone with the Indians to found his new parish. Thus began an abiding relationship between the complex humanistic faith of the Pueblos and the equally complex Catholic faith. As taught by the Franciscans of that period — with their emphasis on brotherly love, human interdependence, and rejection of materialism — Catholicism had much in common with Puelbo values. The Indians, too, believed in a single Creator, in a benevolent mother-figure, in a personal soul that lived after death of the body, and their kachina spirits were very similar to the Catholic belief in the "community of saints." (Among the Navajos, Apaches and Comanches, with a totally different set of beliefs and values, the Franciscan missionaries had virtually no success.)

The alliance was not without its strains. Acoma had been represented at the San Juan meeting only by observers. That winter, eleven members of a patrol visiting the pueblo were killed in a surprise attack. Oñate attacked the mesa-top stronghold, captured it after an epic battle, and sentenced all male prisoners over twenty-five years old to have one foot amputated. Friction also developed quickly between the Franciscans, who accused the military government of misusing the Indians, and the military, who accused the Franciscans of coddling their charges. The first period of colonization along the river was marked by increasing bitterness between church and state, with the Pueblo Indian most often the subject of the quarrel. Governors were excommunicated, priests arrested. Theoretically the argument had been settled in 1537, when Pope Paul III had issued a strongly worded Papal Bull. Satan himself, said the Pope, inspired those Spaniards who declared that Indians should be treated "as dumb brutes created for our service, pretending that they are incapable of receiving the Catholic Faith." The Pope declared that these Indians were not to be deprived of their possessions, or their liberty, even if they did not accept Christianity.

In 1613, just three years after Oñate had moved his capital from near San Juan to the new Royal City of the Holy Faith (Santa Fe), Friar Isidro Ordóñez refused to let Indians of the Taos pueblo deliver a levy of corn to tax collectors sent by Governor Pedro de Peralta. The governor sent troops and collected the corn anyway. Ordóñez denounced the governor for using pressgangs of Indians to build the Palace of Governors at Santa Fe (they built well; after 365 years it is still in use) and excommunicated Peralta. Peralta fired his pistol at the priest, but missed.

Peralta and Ordóñez were replaced, but the conflict continued. It bore bitter fruit.

There were, as there had always been, years of drought and famine. But now the balance of human ecology had changed. The Mescalero Apaches of the mountains, and the Kiowa-Comanches of the plains now had horses. Hungry, they raided the Pueblos with increasing effectiveness and ferocity. The Spanish population by 1670 numbered no more than twenty-five hundred. It could spare an average of no more than four soldiers to guard a pueblo. The so-called Saline pueblos east of the river were abandoned and left to fall to ruins. The Apaches struck at the major river pueblo of Senecu, killed its priest and half its inhabitants. It, too, was abandoned. In the face of this murderous external threat, the Spanish continued their own church-versus-state battle over the treatment of their Indian allies. Then in 1680, the Pueblos took a hand of their own in this dispute.

The revolution was planned at Taos, led by a *cacique* named Popé. On August 10, the northern Pueblos struck in unison — killing the local Spanish and then marching into Santa Fe. Governor Antonio de Otermín and the survivors he could rally held out in the Palace of Governors, and then broke out and fought their way downriver to El Paso, collecting survivors on the way. By autumn the Spanish colony upriver had ceased to exist.

The reconquest came in 1692. The remarkable Don Diego de Vargas led a small army upriver. He found the Indian alliance had collapsed, and with much bluff and diplomacy, reoccupied Santa Fe and obtained the submission of twenty-two pueblos without losing a soldier or killing an Indian. What Otermín had called "the miserable kingdom" was restored. It would survive, in hunger and hardship and constant warfare with Comanche, Apache, and Navajo, until taken by the United States in 1848.

Downriver, the effect of the Europeans was slower in coming. The Franciscans founded a mission at the much-used ford we now call El Paso in 1659. In 1699, Fort John the Baptist and three missions were built at the ford called France Way, three hundred crow-flight miles from the river mouth. San Antonio and a few other small settlements were founded north of the river in the eighteenth century. But the lower river saw little change until the 1820s. In 1821 the flag of Spain came down all along the Rio Grande and was replaced by the banner of an independent Mexico. The same year immigrant colonies of Anglo-Americans were founded in the trans-river territory of Texas. The Spanish government had given a foiled St. Louis banker named Moses Austin permission to settle three hundred families in Texas. The new Mexican government, pre-occupied by its civil war, let the approval stand. It proved to be a fateful decision. That year, 302 years after discovery, there were fewer than three thousand Spanish (now Mexicans) in all of the vast province of the lower Rio Grande. In less than ten years, Moses' sickly son, Stephen, had moved in some fifty-six hundred Anglo-Americans — almost all slaveholding families from Louisiana and other Southern states.

One of the first acts of the Mexican government was to outlaw slavery. In the Coahuila-Texas territory, straddling the Rio Grande, the outraged Texas slaveholders managed first to win an exemption from the decree, and then to have it modified to cover only those born six months after passage of the act. There were other causes of friction, ranging from custom fees to (incredible as it seems in an immense, almost empty country) trouble over land owner-ship between Mexican settlers and immigrants from the U.S. The immigrants proclaimed an independent Republic of Texas, and in the winter of 1833 the Rio Grande saw General Antonio Lopez de Santa Ana, President of Mexico and commander of its army, ferry six thousand troops across to put an end to this treason. Santa Ana wiped out a rebel force defending the Alamo at San Antonio, and won another victory at Goliad. In both places he ordered his reluctant officers to kill all prisoners. Then, at San Jacinto Creek, the Mexican army was routed and Santa Ana captured. The hostage president signed a treaty granting Texas its independence.

That same year, a quieter revolution happened in the old province of Nuevo Mexico. The Franciscan Order, which had been heart and soul of Spanish-Pueblo alliance and source of most of the education upriver, was withdrawn. Secular priests, in theory, replaced the friars. In fact, there were virtually no secular priests, and no financial support to replace the subsidy which had come for generations from the great world-wide Franciscan Order. Within a few years, the churches in many towns, and in most of the pueblos, were standing empty and falling into ruin. Upriver, too, the outside world had been intruding into the isolated Spanish colony. Lieutenant Zebulon Pike had crossed the Front Range of the Rockies in 1808 and camped on the Rio Grande near the mouth of the Conejos. (He pretended when a Spanish patrol came to inquire that he thought it was the Red River.) Pike was escorted downriver to Santa Fe, and eventually to Chihuahua, and then back to Fort John the Baptist to be expelled from the Spanish Territory. He took with him information that in the United States removed the mystery from the Mountain West and the Rio Grande. After Pike, the insatiable Yankee appetite for trade, and a European fad which made hats of beaver fur immensely popular, brought a steady increase in the intrusion of Anglo-Americans into the Spanish-Indian world upriver. The Santa Fe Trail opened, linking Santa Fe with U.S. markets over a road that, while eight hundred miles long, was much easier and quicker than the old Royal Road across mountains and deserts to Mexico City. And the demand for fur brought hundreds of French and Anglo-American trappers swarming into the mountains that rim the river's upper basin. In the thirty years before Chinese silk killed the fur trade, these mountain men made legends in the high country of the San Juans and the Sangre de Cristos. By the late 1820s they were bringing forty thousand pounds of pelts, worth five dollars a pound, out of the mountains each spring. They exterminated the grizzly bear and challenged the mountain Indians for dominion of their territory. When the price of beaver skidded, many remained and added a new element to the culture upriver.

The final great political change came in 1846 to 1848 — affecting the river all along its nineteen hundred miles. The United States annexed the Republic of Texas, war with Mexico flared, and the defeated Santa Ana signed the Treaty of Guadalupe Hidalgo, recognizing the independence of Texas and ceding to the United States its upriver territory and the land from the Gila River to the forty-second parallel and from the Pacific to the Rio Grande. The flag of the United States waved now all along the river. Except for one month in the Civil War era, when Texas joined the Confederacy and carried the Stars and Bars upstream as far as Santa Fe, it would remain. And it would bring to the Great River the overwhelming forces of American civilization — railroads, industrial development, and a flood of immigration. The uneasy joint dominion of Indian tribe and Spanish outpost along the river was ended. The power of the Comanche, Kiowa, Ute, Pawnee, Navajo, and Apache was gradually crushed. And the river itself was measured, allocated, and adjudicated, and — most important — controlled.

The water that pours out of the narrow mouth of the Rio Grande Gorge under the old Taos Junction Bridge has been predicted and allocated long before the snow which produced it melted. It has been gauged repeatedly on its route down the mountain streams and through the myriad irrigation ditches of the San Luis Valley. Under the Lobatos Bridge the pulse of the Rio Grande is taken to determine if Colorado farmers used more than their share of the last winter's snow. When it reaches Otowi Gauge halfway through New Mexico, its volume is gauged again. On a "normal" year, when about a million acre-feet of water run under Otowi Bridge, 53 percent must be delivered into Elephant Butte Reservoir for use in the Juarez-El Paso Valley of Texas-Mexico and in the Mesilla Valley of New Mexico. What these and other gauges report determines whether water must be released, or retained in reservoirs on the tributary streams that feed the great river. In much of the immense Colorado-New Mexico basin, no dams over ten feet high can be built, no water wells drilled, without permission of the state engineer. The right to use water from the river, or the streams that flow into the river, or the moist sands that are supplied by water seeping toward the river, is a valuable property to be bought and sold. It is carefully guarded, and exactly graded—generally on the basis of chronological use. Since the Pueblo Indians were using irrigation water when the Spanish arrived, and their rights were recognized by Spanish law, the Pueblos generally have the senior rights and top priorities. Next come those who hold rights on the old Spanish-colonial ditches. (The Chamita ditch has been irrigating fields since 1724.) On each stream "priorities" are based on location and availability of the ditch to water. And even the individual ditches have their own priorities—the value of each determined by location.

Oddly, where irrigation is oldest on the river it is least important in terms of dollars. The first diversion in the canyon is at Pilar, where the stream is tapped to water the few acres of orchards and vegetable gardens of the old village. Here the canyon widens enough to accommodate U.S. 64-86, and the pavement runs on the bench above the water for thirty miles. The next diversion comes at Velarde, again to water a few hundred acres of apples, peaches, cherries, plums, and fields of chili. At Velarde, the canyon widens toward the Española Valley. Here is the oldest center of civilization in the United States. Each of the little tributary streams that drain the Sangre de Cristo Mountains (named for the "Blood of Christ") is the site of its Spanish colonial village. There is Trampas, Truchas, Santa Cruz, Chimayo, Cundiyo, Cordova, Alcalde, Embudo, and the rest. Most of them were old when George Washington was a boy. They remain, much as they always were—poor adobe buildings, clustered around an adobe church, occupied by families whose names appeared on the roster of Oñate, or of De Vargas. The river itself passes by even older habitations—the pueblo of San Juan, still about the size it was when Oñate established his capital just across the river, and just below the confluence of the Chama, the equally ancient pueblos of Santa Cruz and San Ildefonso.

The Chama is the last of the Rio Grande's major tributaries until the Rio Conchos, almost a thousand miles downstream. Since 1968, part of the contribution it makes to the Great River is water which nature intended for the Colorado River and the Pacific Ocean.

It has been diverted from the water-shed of the San Juan River via a tunnel bored through the Continental Divide. It is dumped into Willow Creek to flow into Heron Reservoir and hence into the Chama. It flows clear, cold, and aswarm with rainbow trout, into the flood control reservoir behind El Vado Dam, and downstream into the flood control dam at Abiquiu, and through the Chama Valley. By now it has dissolved tons of soft, yellow deposits and become sort of muddy orange.

From the San Luis Valley outlet through Española Valley, the Rio Grande drops from 7,440 feet to 5,600. Much of this altitude is lost in the precipitous descent through the gorge. But the canyon from Taos Junction past Pilar to Velarde, and all the way to the Chama, offers boating opportunities which, if less exciting than the gorge, are much more convenient. From the bridge to Pilar, a good dirt road follows the east bank of the river, and the entire strip is a New Mexico state park with picnic and camping facilities. At Pilar the river drops down a five-mile stretch of rapids which are rated an expert Class IV. Near the old wooden Woody Glen Bridge, the Great River is pinched into a narrows (only five feet wide at one point) providing a test of nerve for kayak operators. The fast water ends at the village of Rinconada and for the next thirty miles one can drift effortlessly through the Española Valley, past cottonwood bosques and Indian pueblos and a patchwork of orchards and vegetable gardens.

The next white-water run comes at the end of the valley. The river passes under Otowi Bridge into White Rock Canyon. For twenty-five miles it will wind its way through a narrow cut between the Pajarito and Santa Fe plateaus. It loses about ten feet per mile, which makes for fast water, and its rapids are rated difficult for experienced boaters even at low water.

The scenery here is spectacular — eroded cliffs in which white volcanic pumice is layered with streams of lava. Here Frijoles Creek drains into the river. Up this little stream are the Frijoles cliff dwellings, where ancestors of the present pueblo dwellers lived from the 1200s to about 1550. Why they abandoned the site remains one of anthropology's more baffling mysteries.

At the bottom of the canyon the river pours into Cochiti Reservoir — a massive earth-fill structure completed in 1975 to provide flood and sedimentation control (and a fifty-thousand-acre-foot recreation lake) for the Middle Rio Grande Valley. When filled, the lake will bury most of the rapids of White Rock Canyon — backing water almost to Otowi Bridge.

Downstream from the new dam, the Rio Grande once again becomes a working river. This is the territory of the Keresan-speaking Pueblos, and the river irrigates the fields of the Cochití, Santo Domingo and San Felipe Indians, and pours past the old villages of Algodones and Bernalillo to Albuquerque.

In New Mexico's largest urban area (about three hundred thousand in Greater Albuquerque in the mid-1970s) the Rio Grande manages to affect the city without being affected. It wanders between a high bluff on its west bank and a levee on the east over a broad, sandy bed lined with cottonwoods. It is guarded from population by irrigation ditches and drains that parallel its bed, and insulated from urban affairs by a broad belt of shady bosque. Within a few blocks of the city's downtown business district it provides a strip of natural shady silence still wild enough to attract migrating waterfowl.

The nature of this Middle Rio Grande can best be seen and understood from the crest of Sandia Mountain, which overshadows the river at Albuquerque. From this eleven-thousand-foot ridge, the river is a streak of silver, running through a belt of pale green (gold in autumn, grey in winter) winding through a brown-grey, semi-desert landscape. In the Española Valley, the mountains crowd the river — Sangre de Cristos to the east, and Jemez to the west. Here the western mountains have receded — replaced by the great grassy hump called the plain of Albuquerque. But all through New Mexico and into Texas, mountains dominate the river landscape. Below Albuquerque the great high plain on the west is soon replaced by the Ladron Mountains, the Gallinas, the San Mateos, and finally, the great Black Range, the Mimbres, and the barren Sierra de Uvas, which look down on the Mesilla Valley. To the east the mountain wall is equally ubiquitous. The Sandias give way to the Manzanos, which fade away into the Sierra Oscura and become the hundred-mile-long ridge of the San Andres Mountains.

The Rio Grande meanders down this interwoven trough, its banks shaded by broad cottonwoods, tamarisk and willows and its water depleted to irrigate thousands of small farms that make up the Middle Rio Grande Irrigation District. At Socorro, some eighty miles south of Albuquerque, the basin narrows into the San Marcial marshes. Away from the river, the landscape is what the botanists call Upper Sonoran Desert—the eroded flanks of the hills covered with an infinity of dark green creosote bush and the grey-white desert grasses. Nature, with some help from the U.S. Fish and Wildlife Service, has made this stretch of the Rio Grande a wilderness for birds.

It's called the Bosque del Apache Wildlife Refuge (after the Apaches who used the riverside expanse of cottonwood forest as a staging area for raids upriver). In winter it is home for thousands of snow geese, Canada geese, greater sandhill cranes, clouds of ducks and other waterfowl, and a multitude of other birds in dazzling varieties. At these marshes, the old Royal Road was forced away from the river. For ninety almost waterless miles the old road ran east of a range of low, barren hills on a route the Spanish called Jornada del Muerte (Dead Man's Route). Oñate's colonists blazed this trail, and might have perished on it had not the Tiguex Pueblos sent food to help them.

Out of these narrow marshes the Rio Grande pours into Elephant Butte Reservoir, a forty-mile-long holding basin that waters the rich Mesilla Valley. When completed in 1916, this lake would hold 2,639,000 acre-feet of water. Silting has reduced this capacity, and the Bureau of Reclamation once estimated that by 2016 the huge lake would be filled with topsoil washed downstream. The Cochiti Dam, and other flood control dams on upstream tributaries are now slowing this process. They are also easing the silting problem at Albuquerque, where the bed of the river (behind its levee) is as much as seven feet higher than nearby city streets.

At El Paso, the river simultaneously begins its thousand-mile role as international boundary and passes through its largest urban district—separating the industrial cities of El Paso and Juarez, Mexico. It is dirty here, polluted by use and reuse through hundreds of miles of ditches and drains, and confined to a concrete channel. Before its wandering ways were thus curbed, it had changed its course, and cut the Chamisal district of Juarez off from Mexico— causing years of international friction. Today, the river runs properly north of Chamisal, and Mexico has converted its recovered territory into an eye-catching park-monument to a friendly border. The border has not always been friendly. South of the river lies the state of Chihuahua, the "Mother of Revolutions" in a nation that spent much of its first century engaged in internal strife. Benito Juarez used the Mexican city south of the river (then called El Paso del Norte) as the base of his crusade to free his country from Spanish rule, and to liberate it from the French who replaced the Spanish. Both Francisco Madero and Pancho Villa used it as a base again in the social revolution that gave Mexico its modern republican constitution. The city has been besieged, burned and captured, and more than once bullets have crossed the river to make the streets of El Paso dangerous.

For generations, El Paso streets were made dangerous enough by their own inhabitants. The Treaty of Guadalupe Hidalgo split the little settlement on the river ford into U.S. and Mexican towns and made both sides a convenient hangout for fugitives. When it was incorporated in 1873, El Paso had a total population of 173 citizens. But the Southern Pacific, Santa Fe, Texas Pacific and the Mexican Central railroads all connected into the community in 1881 and 1882, restoring its role as an international crossroads and bringing it a flood of citizens (including John Wesley Hardin, whom legend credits with killing twenty-six men—six more than Billy the Kid) and a widespread reputation as the gambling and sin center of the Southwest. In 1910, the city prohibited gambling and dance halls and since the 1920s, its economy has been based on agriculture, ore smelting, international trade, and Fort Bliss, the base from which the United States Army trains antiaircraft and artillery missile personnel on desert test ranges that extend some two hundred miles into New Mexico.

Perhaps no place along its nineteen hundred miles has the Rio Grande been so altered by man as at this famous crossing. Its length has been cut by concrete channels that reduce 150 miles of meandering bends to less than 90 miles. The river, which had been described as "a mile wide, a foot deep, too thin to plow and too thick to drink, always flooding, and always changing beds," now passes through the El Paso-Juarez corridor as orderly and predictable as plumbing.

But here the Rio Grande, as we have seen it from its source at Stony Pass, has about played out its string. At Fort Quitman, the El Paso-Juarez Valley narrows and the last irrigation drain trickles what remains of its water back into the river. As far as those who manage the Rio Grande Interstate Compact are concerned, the river that drains the Southern Rockies is finished. It has come almost seven hundred miles and irrigated almost a million acres, and used up more than nine thousand feet of altitude. At Fort Quitman, the river is only thirty-four hundred feet above sea level, with twelve thousand miles still to travel before it reaches the Gulf.

For the next hundred miles, the depleted Rio Grande runs through the narrow, desert valley between the barren Quitman Mountains of Texas and Chihuahua's waterless Sierra del Huesco. On the U.S. side, the highway quits the river country at Fort Hancock. On the Mexican side, the farm road that has wandered down through a rosary of bosque villages (San Augustin, Guadalupe, Bravos, San Ignacio, Nuevo, and Cedillos) fades to nothing at Banderas. Along the river there are a few desert willows and tamarisk. Otherwise it is a dead landscape of stone and cacti — uninhabited on both sides of the border for almost a hundred miles. Only reptiles live in this landscape, and those few mammals which — like the kangaroo rat — can live without drinking. And then, just above the place where an international bridge links Presidio, Texas, with the ancient adobe town of Ojinaga, Mexico, the Rio Conchos appears, like a miracle out of the stony desert, and pours a transfusion of cold, clear water into the Rio Grande. The Franciscan, Fray Agustín Rodriquez, found this place in 1581 while exploring for souls to save. Finding a few Indians here, the Misión del Apostól Santiago was built to convert them — and later the Presidio to protect the mission from Comanches. Forty miles below this historic "Junta del Rios," the revived Great River squanders much of what altitude is left of it, roaring through three of America's most spectacular canyons. Here, sometime in the Cenozoic era, a series of geologic paroxysms bent and folded the earth's crust and produced a ragged cluster of mountains, the Sierra del Consuelo, the Sierra Carmen in Mexico and the Chisos in Texas. Through them, the river is forced southward into "The Big Bend" and through the awesome, twisting slots called Santa Elena, Mariscal, and Boquillas canyons.

As in the Rio Grande gorge, the river here is walled by immense, vertical cliffs, but the Big Bend canyons are very different from the gorge. The river below Lobatos Bridge seems to sink into a black lava earth. Here, below the ford at the village of Lajitas, the earth seems to rise skyward around the river. At the upper end of Santa Elena Canyon, the river slides silently toward the immense limestone upthrust of Mesa de Anguila, which rises almost eighteen hundred feet above water level. The river flows through a slot in this formation. A mile inside it encounters the Big Bend country's most dangerous rapids, the "Rockslide." The Rio Grande pours through a jumble of great polished boulders and is considered lethal, even for the experts, in high water. Much of the float through all three canyons, however, is relatively easy at lower water, and much different from the black gorge in New Mexico. Here, cliffs and boulders are more often limestone white than basalt black, the canyon is generally much wider at the bottom, the cliffs higher and more vertical, the water warm and murky instead of cold and clear, and the endless thunder of the gorge rapids replaced by an eerie silence. And, instead of a continuous cut of fifty miles, the Big Bend canyons are separated by open country. Marisal Canyon is almost fifty miles of open desert below Santa Elena and, like Santa Elena, a narrow, twisting slot walled in by limestone cliffs. They rise, like skyscrapers from a street, from fifteen hundred to eighteen hundred feet.

For a hundred miles east of the Big Bend country, the river passes through empty desert — past the treeless, waterless ridges of the Sierra del Carmen and the margin of the vast Edwards Plateau. Before it reaches the communities of Del Rio and Ciudad Acuña where it is joined in the Amistad Reservoir by the Pecos and Devils rivers, the Rio Grande has gone through almost three hundred miles of isolation, unbridged and, except for Big Bend Park roads, difficult to reach. Now its character changes again. It slides past the hill country of Texas and, for the first time since Fort Quitman, it irrigates a rich valley. The land flattens, and the climate subtly changes. At Del Rio, the river bed is only 950 feet above sea level. Where it flows under the bridge linking Laredo and Nuevo Laredo it has 440 feet of altitude left. The countryside here is flat — cactus and mesquite country were not reclaimed by irrigation canals. The Gulf of Mexico is still 350 miles downstream but its climate is already affecting the river.

There is humidity in the air now, and a sense of mildness. The cycle of the river is also changed. Its heavy runoff season has shifted from the spring of mountain snowmelts to the late-summer and autumn of Gulf Coast rainstorms.

The largest reservoir on the river, a three-million-acre-foot lake behind the Falcon Dam, controls the final 150 miles of the river and waters one of the richest river deltas this side of the Nile. Falcon Lake is also fed by the Rio Salado and Rio Sabinas and provides a steady diet of water for almost a million acres of citrus groves and cropland on both sides of the border. The river is bigger here. It was on this strip that Captain Henry Austin's steamship "Ariel" hauled cargo and passengers for his cousin's new colony in the 1820s. (Austin could take his paddlewheeler as far west as Roma even at low water.) It is still, in many places, lined by the palms for which Piñeda named it. But here it has run out of altitude. Much of its irrigation water is lifted from its ditches by pumps. It flows past Rio Grande City, Mission, Reynosa and finally under the bridges that link Brownsville with that historic gateway-to-Mexico, Matamoros. It is now a tropical river, a tidewater river. As the seabirds fly, it is only thirty miles to the Gulf of Mexico. But through this pool-table flatness the Rio Grande wanders a hundred miles before it finally delivers its muddy surplus to the sea.

Rio Grande, Spruce Forest, David Muench

Rio Grande, Sierra Blanca, David Muench

Rio Grande, Sandia Mountains, Robert Reynolds

Rio Grande, Northern New Mexico Canyon, David Muench

Rio Grande, San Elizario, Robert Reynolds

Rio Grande, Big Bend Cliffs, Robert Reynolds

Rio Grande, Church in Los Ebanos, Robert Reynolds

Rio Grande, Burros, Robert Reynolds

Places for Spirits, Ship Rock, David Muench

From Albuquerque, the California-bound Amtrak detours down the shady bosque of cottonwoods lining the Rio Grande. It crosses the river at Isleta Pueblo and climbs the long slope we locals call "the llano." If I am a passenger, it's about then that I move up to the observation car. When the train tops the ridge I will enjoy a scene which never fails to move me. From this ridge you look into a land full of spirits.

The last time I saw into America's very own Holy Land from an Amtrak observation car it was late summer—the last days of the thunderstorm season. I sat near three men who had boarded days before somewhere far east of Chicago and had formed the sort of friendship train travel encourages. When the Amtrak reached the crest and the emptiness of western New Mexico opened before us, their conversation stopped mid-sentence. "My God!" one said. "Why would anyone live out here?"

Why, indeed?

We saw hundreds of square miles of dry country, eight inches of rain on a wet year, an infinity of needle grass, grama, snakeweed and rabbit brush; tan and grey, freckled here and there with the dark green of junipers, streaked and dappled with cloud shadows. Beyond this great bowl of prairie rose the shapes of Noer Butte, Chicken Mountain and—dim blue with distance—the Zuni range where Spider Grandmother led the Zunis to the Center of the Universe. There are the Cebollitos, Mesa Gigante where the Lagunas have their villages, and—looming above them all—the Turquoise Mountain of the Navajos. It is an arid landscape, inhospitable, almost empty, with none of the lush green which spells riches and prosperity. It is built far out of human scale, too large for habitation, making man feel tiny, threatened, aware of his fragil mortality.

Perhaps that is why it is good for me, why I seem to need it, and return at every excuse. As I cross the ridge and see the Turquoise Mountain looming on the horizon, the weight of Albuquerque, of the buzzing telephone, of unanswered mail and unkept promises falls away. It is my favorite mountain, and the gateway to my favorite places.

One of them is on the mountain itself. We call it Mount Taylor. For the Tewa-speaking Pueblo Indians of the Rio Grande, it is Dark Mountain where the two Little War Gods sometimes dwell. For the Navajos it is Tsodzil, one of the four mountains which mark the corners of Diné Bikeyah—Navajo Country. It was built in its present form in this Navajo "Fifth World" by the spirit called First Man. But it had also existed in the earlier worlds through which the Navajos had evolved toward humanity, culture and harmony. First Man built it on a magic blue blanket, then pinned it to the earth with his knife to keep it from floating away. He made it beautiful with turquoise and assigned Blue Flint Girl to live on Mosca Peak, guarded forever by Big Snake, and forever guarding the Navajos from chaos.

I can see the Turquoise Mountain from my Albuquerque home. It rises on the horizon—a ragged indigo line against the garish sunsets, snowcapped in winter, wearing a scarf of blowing clouds in the windy spring, forming the base for towering thunderstorms in the summer. When smog fills the Rio Grande Valley, it seems to float above the earth as if First Man's magic knife had slipped. It is only sixty-five miles away but it reminds me of a different world.

My favorite place on that mountain is easy to reach—a fast drive west on Interstate 40 to Grants, then State Road 547 into the San Mateo Mountains and upward on the forest service road to the Mosca Peak lookout. Long ago a fire swept through the forest here, leaving a jackstraw jumble of fallen timbers. Aspen and mountain mahogany have grown up through that woodpile now, young fir and spruce are making their comeback, and the meadows opened by the burn are blue and yellow with wild iris, columbine and lupine. It is one of the places I have memorized. I can visit it by merely closing my eyes.

Navajo shaman come here to collect minerals for their "four mountains jish" and herbs for their medicine bundle. You sometimes see the painted stick-and-feather prayer plumes they leave as offerings for what they have taken. It was here in Navajo mythology that Monster Slayer and Born for Water, his thoughtful twin brother, killed Walking Giant with arrows of lightning. It is here that Father Sky touches his hand to that of Mother Earth.

I like to come on summer afternoons when the Turquoise Mountain is playing its role as mother of the thunderstorms. Last August I sat on a log watching the drifting mist erase the forest around me, recreate it, then hide it again. The rumble and thump of thunder in the surrounding cloud could have been the remembered sound of the epic struggle of Walking Giant and Monster Slayer. Then the storm moved eastward leaving silence behind. A faint breeze brought in the smell of rain and forest dampness and the sound of a horned lark somewhere out there in the mist, and the sorrowful call of a saw-whet owl. I found myself forgetting the violent Odyssey of the Hero Twins and remembering another piece of Navajo mythic poetry. It teaches that to shelter Blue Flint Girl on this peak, First Man built "a house made of morning mist, a house made of dawn." On a day like that it was easy to believe that the holy girl still lives in such a house, just out of sight behind the firs, keeping her eternal promise to preserve harmony.

This empty, impoverished country west of Albuquerque holds many such places for me. Below the mountain, for example, is the *malpais,* some eighty thousand acres of lava badlands produced by eruptions of this old volcano. The Navajos call it "Ye'iitsoh Bidil," or Monster's Blood, and their origin mythology makes it the congealed black blood of the ogre killed on the mountain. Traditional Navajos tend to avoid the lava, but to the neighboring Acoma Indians it is holy ground and a place where prayer sticks are left to the kachina spirits.

Interstate 40 crosses the north end of the malpais making it easy for those of us who enjoy such weirdness to find isolation in a surreal landscape. An old road wanders southwestward from the Interstate toward the village of Fence Lake. Anyone who likes to be alone can park beside that road, walk out into the lava, and have the planet to himself.

The malpais was formed by a series of lava flows over eons of time. Some are worn smooth by a million years and colored by layers of lichens. Some are as recent as five hundred years ago and are still raw and ragged. Water falling here has no place to sink. It collects in potholes, and bubbles up in springs where reeds grow and birds nest. The rodents and reptiles attracted by these little water holes take on the camouflage of a lava universe. Kangaroo rats and field mice here are black instead of tan, and lizards are sooty grey — thus less visible to the golden eagles and hawks hunting overhead.

At midsummer, the malpais is indeed "bad country." The high altitude sun makes the basalt too hot to touch, and the rattle-snakes are on the prowl for rodents. But on winter days, anyone who enjoys offbeat sensations can find them safely amid the lava. The solitude is absolute. A short tramp from the old road takes you to places where you can stare in every direction and see no sign that earth is inhabited. Add the surrealism of the lava — like an ocean of black ink frozen mid-storm — and one can imagine himself stranded in some lost galaxy.

I have been prowling this empty corner of the Southwest for much of my life — the first twenty years simply because it appealed to me, and the next twenty because I use it as the setting of the novels I write about Navajos. Thus I have collected a variety of places which lift my spirit. Another of these is another Navajo sacred place. Ship Rock.

The Navajos call it *Tse' Bit'a'i'* — The Rock With Wings. It's the basaltic core of volcano, once protected by a great cone of ash. Now with the cone eroded away, the basalt throat rises out of an ocean of prairie grass like a Gothic cathedral built for giants. Its peak is 7,178 feet above sea level, and while that is lower than the Chuska Mountains just west on the Arizona border, the Chuska are normal mountains. Ship Rock isn't. It soars out of the earth, twenty stories taller from its grassy base than the World Trade Center towers are from the Manhattan pavements.

On the spire of this monolith, Monster Slayer almost met his match. After killing the Winged Monster and persuading the monster's nestlings to become the eagle and the owl, he found there was no way down. Spider Grandmother pitied him, finally, and lowered him to earth. The spire's sheer cliffs also attracted modern climbers until the Navajo Tribal Council declared this holy place off limits to desecrating sportsmen.

I am attracted less by the spire and more by a related oddity. The same volcanism which produced the mountain produced three long cracks in the earth's shell. Through these, melted magma was forced up like toothpaste into the layer of ash the volcano had deposited. The same eons which eroded away Ship Rock's cone exposed these "rays." They extend miles from the central core, incredibly thin black walls. I miss no chance to reassure myself that they're as remarkable as I remember them.

Navajo Route 33, en route to Red Rock and the Lukachukai Mountains, crosses a gap in the most impressive of these rays. At the gap, the wall is about two or three feet thick, perhaps twenty feet high. Here and there, blocks of basalt have fallen out leaving unlikely portholes. A track leaves the road in this gap and meanders along the foot of the talus below the wall. I walked down the top of the talus last November. It was twilight on a day when a weather front was bulging southward out of Utah, the sky had its stormy look and the air smelled of snow. The wind was gusty, now hooting through the wall's ragged windows, now subsiding to a sigh. A sparrow hawk was balanced on the currents above, looking for a careless mouse. The basalt ray undulated southward, uphill and down, like a black and narrow version of the Great Wall of China. At its end, the spires of Ship Rock were black against the sky.

That monolith and that once-plastic wall always remind me of the force that cracked the earth there and pushed that molten rock upward. They are thoughts to put the triviality of the human species in perspective.

Other places and other moments stick in my memory.

Bosque del Apache Wildlife Refuge down the Rio Grande from Socorro, with the red January dawn outlining the Oscura Mountains. Suddenly a sound, growing rapidly: the awakening of scores of thousands of waterfowl wintering there: snow geese, awakening Canada geese, awakening sandhill cranes, awakening the mallards and the teal and the pintails. Then the air filling with geese, rising in a kaleidoscope of shifting formations, soaring high enough to be caught by the slanting sunlight, forming patterns against the grey velvet of the Coyote Hills, turning upriver toward you. In a moment the sky overhead is white with an infinity of geese. You hear nothing but their excited conversations. You look through a crack in time and glimpse how it was before the white man came.

Canyon de Chelly is another place which provokes the imagination into time travel. The canyon is filled with reminders of the people who occupied it for a thousand years and then faded away—leaving behind a wonderful supply of unanswered questions about where they went, and why, and why they never returned. Across the canyon from one of the cliff houses they abandoned, a trail leads down some six hundred feet from the rim to the sandy floor of Chinle Wash. You can wade across the shallow stream there (giving yourself a cheap thrill if you like by dabbling in the quicksand for which the place is famous) and reach the site we call White House Ruin. It was abandoned about eight hundred years ago by the people the Navajos named Anasazi (actually, *anaasa'zi,'* or "ancestors of enemy people"). Below it is a little bosque of cottonwoods where I like to loaf.

It was here twenty-five years ago that the plot idea jelled for my first book—causing a fictional archaeologist to be trapped deep in just such a canyon and to escape captivity by knowing exactly how cliff dwellers built their houses. It was in this canyon that I first saw an Anasazi pictograph of Kokopela, a flute-playing version of Pan. And it was here one evening that I heard what seemed to be Kokopela's flute. It was faint at first, high notes rising and falling, coming nearer down the canyon and defying any but mythological explanations. Then a goat appeared around the canyon bend and with him, alas, came mundane reality. A flock was following him, many wearing bells. The echo of the cliffs blended the tinkling into a single song.

These pink sandstone cliffs are coated with tough, dark deposits of manganese oxide—the desert varnish which nature seems to have created for artists—and the Anasazis covered a lot of it with their drawings. You see human forms with horns, with torsos decorated with handprints, with the feet of birds. You see oddly inhuman shapes holding hands, or linking arms, or armless. There are snakes, cryptic abstractions and even a depiction which might explain what happened to these people—figures using lances and throwing sticks in combat with figures using bows—a more deadly weapon which the Anasazis seem never to have mastered. Kokopela is everywhere, with his humpback and his little round head, in various shapes, forms, and positions—but always playing what looks like a clarinet. The Navajos have added him to their pantheon of spirits, calling him Water Sprinkler and making his hump a sack of seeds, and of troubles.

The Hopis who occupied this canyon later and know the Anasazis as their ancestors, also left their pictographs, as did the Navajos who arrived later still. Hopi art is mostly abstract—clans' totems and symbolic representations from their migration stories. Navajo artists were more pragmatic. At the Standing Cow site there's a life-sized cartoon of a cow. Pale against the dark red stone up the canyon rides a column of men wearing wide-brimmed hats and carrying muskets. This column of Mexican troops came in 1805 and slaughtered scores of Navajos who had taken refuge up-canyon in what is now aptly called Massacre Cave. Kit Carson, with his militia and his Ute allies, rode into the canyon some sixty years later and repeated the slaughter.

It is particularity quiet in the canyon in the winter. Navajo families who summer there have moved back to their homes on Defiance Plateau and tourist season has ended. The branch canyon (Del Muerto), where the structure called the Tower is built is narrow and the streaked cliffs soar toward a narrow slot of sky. On the sandy floor twilight comes early, but the sun still lights the top of the cliff. Archaeologists say the last log used in an Anasazi structure was cut in the year 1284 and used in the Tower. They believe it was built by refugees who had abandoned the stone apartments at Mesa Verde. But as soon as they built it, something happened here, too, and their civilization ended between these great red cliffs.

What happened? I can lean against the cold cliff here in the premature twilight and watch the darkness move up the cliff as the sun sets and think about these refugees. These artists, these builders, these religious people, seemed to have this side of the planet mostly to themselves. From what, then, were they fleeing? From what was the Tower built to defend them? What finally ended their civilization?

The Navajos have a story for that as they do for everything. (Canyon de Chelly, for example, was created when Water Monster released a flood to force Coyote to return his kidnapped baby.) In the Navajo Wind Way legend, the Anasazi were the Blessed Ones. The Holy People had given them all the arts, from pottery and weaving to corn and the domestication of animals, and taught them the Wind Way ceremonial to cure their illnesses. But the Anasazi became lazy and fell from grace. Illness came and they began misusing the Wind Way. This produced an immense fiery whirlwind which swept them away and left the cliffs streaked and stained.

That explains why Navajo shaman use the Wind Way only as prescribed — to cure illnesses of mind and spirit. Perhaps it explains why so few burials are found around the Anasazi ruins. And the story, and a thousand stories like it, explains why I come to this country when I feel the need for spirits, and to this canyon when I feel a need for ghosts.

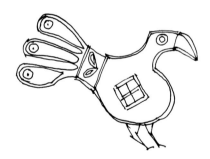

Places for Spirits, La Ventana Arch in Cibolla Wilderness, David Muench

Places for Spirits, Cliff House in Tyuonyi Ruin, David Muench

Places for Spirits, Indian Corn, Robert Reynolds

Places for Spirits, Petroglyph, Robert Reynolds